Accountable Kids

Raising Accountable Kids
One Step at a Time

Scott W. Heaton
Traci S. Heaton

Illustrated by: Rene Sundberg

Timeless Treasures

Rene Sundberg, Educational & Creative Consultant

Accountable Kids Kit graphics and logo © by Kim Holt and Rene Sundberg

Cover watercolor by Alyxandra, Emily, and Sarah Heaton

Visit our web site at Http://www.accountablekids.com

Timeless Treasures
Second edition
www.timelesstreasurespublishing.com
Printed in the United States of America

ISBN 0-9754425-0-3

Dedicated to our children for bringing joy to our days, passion to our work, and purpose to our lives.

Acknowledgements

"If I have seen farther than others, it is because I was standing on the shoulders of giants." Isaac Newton

We have stood on the shoulders of many giants in the conception, creation, and production of the *Accountable Kids* program. To them, we give our love, appreciation, and heartfelt gratitude.

A special thank you from our hearts goes to Rene Sundberg for sharing the journey of developing *Accountable Kids*. Her help, inspiration, and guidance made our dreams a reality. She wove life into our ideas with her artistic abilities, intuitive words, educational expertise, and endless support. Her time and talents have guided this book from its conception to its completion.

We wish to thank Lisa Hains Barker, Ph.D; Dan Sanderson, Ph.D; Matt Eschler, LMFT; and Jonette Reber, LMFT for sharing their expertise in the field of psychology. Their discussions, editing, and ideas have helped us develop a comprehensive program with depth and breadth.

Many others deserve thanks and appreciation. We are indebted to Andrea Schmutz and Kent Sundberg for helping us clarify, organize, and simplify our book with their editing expertise; our family and friends who have contributed to, used, and tested our program; and our brothers and sisters for their encouragement, help, and unwavering enthusiasm.

We appreciate the support and helpful comments from the many friends and family who have implemented the *Accountable Kids* program in their home. We especially want to express our gratitude to Troy and Heidi Heaton, Lisa and Kelly Findlay, Michelle and Gunter Nobis, Miriam and Adam Hughes, and Jerry and J.J. Seare for their suggestions, support, and encouragement.

Our sincere appreciation and thanks go to Kim Holt for her artistic talents, Dr. Bill & Deberah Seare for their support and enthusiasm, Trent Keller and Suzanne Wallis for their constructive criticisms and helpful suggestions, Joe Alter for producing professional advertising in record time, Shonnie Barlow for promoting our program and believing in our abilities from the beginning, Chuck Mazlow for his design abilities, Trent Kenworthy for transforming our ideas into reality, Chris Heinrich for her awesome laser etching, Justin McEwan for going the extra mile during the printing of our book, and Bret Nybo for his incredible talents in web design. Our final thank you goes to our parents Rene Sundberg, Kent Sundberg, and Darol & Georgia Heaton for teaching us a core sense of values and encouraging us to always pursue our dreams.

Contents

Step 2

Step 3

Step 4

Foreword

Most people discover that becoming parents changes their priorities and the way they view the world. While raising children can be joyful and fulfilling, the responsibilities associated with parenting can provoke a great deal of anxiety. As parents, we want our children to grow up to become happy, secure, successful adults, but we may feel inadequately prepared to accomplish these goals. Most parents spend time thoughtfully contemplating aspects of parenting, such as how to improve the quality of family life, how to transmit cultural and spiritual values, and how to best educate their children for social and vocational success. The *Accountable Kids* program is the result of such contemplation. It was developed by parents who prioritized quantity and quality time with their children. It is based on an accumulation of real parenting experiences, consideration of child development, and clinical experience.

What started as a personal, structured means to acquire family peace and teach important values, worked so well that it was expanded and shared with others. The *Accountable Kids* program was tested by many families to ensure it was adaptable to children of different ages, with varying backgrounds and temperaments. The organization of the program is sound and is based on established theories of learning and behavior modification. In fact, most psychologists and therapists who work with children have some version of a behavior modification program they commonly recommend to help eliminate unwanted behavior and provide incentives for more healthy behavioral responses.

To say the *Accountable Kids* program is based on a behavior modification program, though, is like comparing a full-course Thanksgiving feast to a left-over turkey sandwich. In *Accountable Kids*, the quick fix of a typical behavior modification program has been transformed into a dynamic, comprehensive parenting plan that encourages parents to be thoughtful, active agents in the process of rearing their children. *Accountable Kids* not only focuses on extinguishing behavioral problems, it is a developmentally-based program that allows children to learn about choices, accountability, consequences, and important life values. It is also a ready-to-implement source of structure and organization that can be used to help families work together smoothly and less stressfully.

All children feel more secure when grounded in a structured daily routine. The *Accountable Kids* program is well-suited for children. Speaking from my experience as a psychologist, the program may be particularly appealing to stressed mothers and fathers who struggle to parent difficult children. Children are born with important differences in temperament, physical energy, and learning styles. Children who have difficulty understanding consequences of their behavior, children who are impulsive, who have high energy levels, or who are less compliant than their peers, may benefit from the repetition, emphasis on immediate consequences, and organization that the *Accountable Kids* program provides. The same is true for children who have been diagnosed with Attention Deficit Disorder/Attention Deficit Hyperactivity Disorder. Children with these characteristics, or other difficult-to-parent children, can leave parents feeling frustrated and angry.

Accountable Kids provides a way for parents to discipline children consistently (taking Tickets), with less likelihood of losing control, yelling, or expressing anger in other potentially damaging ways. The *Accountable Kids* program may also be helpful for busy, tired parents who find themselves falling into ineffective parenting habits, such as an over-reliance on television or video games to keep children entertained. It may also assist those parents who have difficulty consistently enforcing rules. All of these challenges are addressed in the *Accountable Kids* program.

With appropriate tools from *Accountable Kids* to address problem behaviors efficiently and effectively, parents will likely have more time and energy to strengthen emotional bonds with their children. Strained parent/child relationships can be repaired. Instead of spending all their parenting time addressing problem behaviors, parents can help their children discover talents and abilities and can teach them positive skills and values necessary to live independently. The *Accountable Kids* program is applicable for children age four through teens. It can also be simplified and adapted for three year-olds.

Children need parents' guidance and love. The *Accountable Kids* program provides a solid framework or structure on which to base parenting. It is an organized, practical approach to meet the challenges of raising children. But it is the parents that provide the energy, love, and creativity that invigorate the program. If parents creatively apply the program to their child's individual needs and are willing to be flexible and spend the time necessary to make it work, I believe the *Accountable Kids* program can substantially improve the quality of family relationships and strengthen children to meet the challenges of the future confidently and successfully.

Lisa Hains Barker, Ph.D.
Clinical Psychologist

Introduction

Children are blessings . . .
to be guided by us and then allowed to fly free,
expressing their own unique individuality.

Why use the Accountable Kids program? Because it works! This is a unique parenting program that is parent friendly, easy to use, and effective for children of all ages. The Accountable Kids program has been designed to help you be successful and empowered in your parenting. The formula for developing accountability is presented in a simple format which enables you to aid your children in developing accountability and transform the quality of your relationships with them. The program contains powerful tools to help you change your children's behavioral patterns and encourage positive development and growth.

Being a part of the Accountable Kids creation process with my daughter and son-in-law has been a rewarding and exciting adventure. As a mother, grandmother, and educator, I see a great need for children to learn to be responsible and accountable in the home, at school, and in public life. As a teacher, I have seen many children with low self-esteem, who do not have the self-confidence necessary to allow them to rise to their full potential. They are unaware of the many talents and abilities they possess and feel dependent and unable to direct their lives.

You can help your child soar by teaching the principles presented in the Accountable Kids program. The lessons learned establish a solid foundation that can be relied on later as your child encounters life's storms. They provide concrete stepping stones to help your child develop qualities necessary to become a successful adult. As you implement the steps in the program, you will learn to make healthy parenting choices, teach important life skills, strengthen your family as a whole, and, best of all, experience more fun together as a family!

The Accountable Kids program is based on the principle of the law of the harvest: you reap what you sow. The program allows your child to experience this principle on a continuing basis through choices and consequences. It is designed to foster positive behaviors and eliminate negative behaviors, enabling your child to feel valuable and empowered. The program allows your child to sow his own garden and be rewarded, or not rewarded, by his own efforts.

". . . for whatsoever a man soweth, that shall he also reap." Galatians 6:7 KJV

Rural America lived the law of the harvest. When our forefathers settled America, children were a very important part of family life. All family members participated in supporting the family, and all efforts were vital to its success. The family unit encompassed parents, grandparents, aunts, uncles, children, and grandchildren, all living together in the same community. Everyone was responsible to help sustain the family. As children grew older, they worked alongside adults or began apprenticeships, becoming productive members of society. Children were considered a valuable commodity because of the role they played. They were participating members of the family unit, and because of this, they developed self esteem and felt valued as they contributed to the family's welfare.

In contrast today, it is common to see children and adolescents feeling isolated from the family and society, taking, but giving very little in return. Many do not experience the joy, satisfaction, and feeling of self worth that come from effort, achievement, hard work, and being a part of something larger than themselves. Because of this, many children have been deprived of the gifts and abilities that come along with working and achieving.

Most parents desire to make their children responsible and accountable, but often they are not certain how to do this. Accountability and responsibility become vague ideas, wonderful to contemplate, but seemingly impossible to implement. Children learn negative behaviors, and parents are unsure how to curb them and encourage positive behaviors. This is the reason the Accountable Kids program was developed. It is a dynamic "how to" that takes the guesswork out of parenting.

The program was designed to be simple and enjoyable to use, bringing consistency, balance, and harmony into your home. It was intended to form a basis for your own creativity and specific personal manner of parenting. The colorful graphics and tickets make it a visually enjoyable program for children of any age.

Having an accountable, responsible child may sound too good to be true, but the truth is, it is possible! As you implement the program, your child will experience the result of his actions and gain a feeling of empowerment and self-confidence from knowing he is in control of many of the areas of his life. It will require effort and consistency to keep the program running until new behaviors are learned and fresh habits are ingrained, but when you see your child responsibly thriving, the reward will be worth all the time and effort you put forth.

The Accountable Kids program is the result of countless generations passing down their knowledge, wisdom, common sense, and values. Those who have gone before stand in the wings, whispering messages of hope and encouragement. The responsibility is now ours to love, to nurture, and to teach the values and ideals we would like our children to exemplify. We teach by example, by loving consistently, by responsible direction, and by commendable actions.

The Accountable Kids program has developed into something greater than the individuals involved. It is a divinely inspired program containing heart, soul, and depth.

It was directed and inspired by God. His hand has been the guiding force, His love has been the prime directive, and His message the ultimate goal. This book is His miracle.
Thank you God!

*"For of him, and through him, and to him, **are** all things: to whom be glory for ever. Amen."*
Romans 11:36 KJV

Rene Sundberg, M.Ed.
Educational & Creative Consultant

Back to Basics

The *Accountable Kids* program combines valuable parenting principles with external tools to help children internalize positive behaviors and values. Children learn to take responsibility for their actions and begin to govern, trust, and love themselves. The *Accountable Kids* (*AK*) program is designed to strengthen relationships between parents and children and build a foundation for growth, success, and happiness. Children learn that successful adults govern their lives by the same principles.

Children participating in the *AK* program feel appreciated and cared for as they experience positive interactions, learning that parents are there for support

1

and guidance. Children begin to view themselves as vital components of the family and develop confidence and self worth by becoming contributing members. They experience the family as a place of safety, consistency, and opportunity.

Steps to Accountability

> Children gain knowledge of what is expected.
> Children learn basic responsibility and work ethics by completing chores.
> Privileges are earned by completing basic chores.
> Children experience the benefits of working toward future incentives.
> Parents acknowledge positive behaviors.
> Negative behaviors are extinguished by encouraging alternate positive behaviors.
> Incentives are given *intermittently* to sustain behavior.
> Values are instilled through life lessons and positive reinforcements.
> Children experience the benefits of saving and planning.
> The family learns to work together, plan ahead, and solve problems in the Family Forum.
> Children and parents become skilled at exploring interests, relaxing, and rejuvenating.

A Program with Depth

The *Accountable Kids* program is not a reward system that teaches children to grow up expecting something for every action. Instead, children learn that rewards come at different times and in different ways. The final goal is for children to discover that some of the most important rewards come from within.

The *AK* program uses life lessons of completing jobs, earning privileges, displaying positive behaviors, and working for future rewards to develop positive character traits. Parents also learn how children think, reason, and learn through fun experiments and simple psychological theories.

Simple techniques and valuable concepts are presented to help parents eliminate nagging and continual directing. Through mastering the principles in the *AK* program, children will develop self-confidence and a feeling of accomplishment.

CONFIDENCE!

"My thirteen-year old son was diagnosed with Attention Deficit Hyperactivity Disorder (AD/HD). We have been using the Accountable Kids program for three months and have been experiencing wonderful improvements, but yesterday I received news I just had to share.

Parent teacher conferences have always been a distressing and frustrating time for us. It is so heartbreaking to continually

hear that our son is struggling academically and socially. As the conference began, I prepared for the worst. The teacher looked at me and began to smile. He said he didn't know what we were doing that was different, but our son was now more confident, happy, and making great academic strides. He presented a positive report card showing my son's grades had increased dramatically.

We knew the AK program was helping our son at home, but we didn't expect a change of this magnitude at school. The program has helped him to feel better about himself and improved his self-confidence. Before we began the program, we were focused on all the areas where he needed improvement, and we overlooked all the positive things he was accomplishing.

The Accountable Kids program allowed us to acknowledge and encourage our son's positive behaviors, and it helped him take responsibility for his  *negative actions. Because of the constant positive reinforcement he received in the AK program, his confidence in all areas improved." K.F.*

The *Accountable Kids* program offers effective ways to discipline. Children learn that their choices have consequences. The *AK* program changes the idea of discipline into self-discipline. These concepts closely model the consequences adults encounter.

Using the *AK* program, parents and children learn to maximize their time and efforts. Children learn exactly what is expected and understand the consequences of not fulfilling their obligations. The *AK* program provides structure and harmony to a busy household by shifting responsibility from parents to children. This frees up time and resources for everyone.

"I have never written to a company before, but I wanted you to know how much the Accountable Kids program has changed our life. My children are completing the same chores they did before we began the program, but now they are acknowledged for their efforts. They have become a helpful part of our family. They are willing participants and excited to contribute. Now, when my children say 'thank you', there is real appreciation in their voices.

I always thought my children felt a part of our family, but they have expressed how much better it is to be involved in the rules and consequences. The Family Forum provides a time to plan ahead and make changes in our  *routine. The lines of communication are open and our good relationships have gotten even better. The program has given me a way to nip negative behaviors in the bud before they become habits. My children seem to have more confidence and self esteem because we are focusing on the positive things they do." M.H.*

Empowerment

Accountable Kids are empowered children. They learn to make decisions, engage in positive behaviors, and limit idle activities. Accountable Kids have the ability to work and earn privileges and luxuries. Children experience free agency and develop the ability to direct their lives through choice.

Children learn to direct behaviors towards positive outcomes rather than negative ones. They become empowered as they connect actions with consequences and feel the joy and power that come through accountability and self-reliance. This process develops self-control and self-discipline in a loving and directed manner.

The Positive Aspects of Failure

The *Accountable Kids* program is designed to help children develop into responsible adults by teaching principles of accountability at a young age. The program allows for success, failure, consequences, learning, and growth.

It is important to allow children to be responsible for their actions. Although it is difficult to watch children experience undesirable consequences, this process is critical in teaching responsibility and accountability. Real learning and growth come when children are allowed to make choices and then experience the consequences.

Parents who are overly protective and do not allow their children to experience failure, deprive them of opportunities to grow and learn valuable life lessons. Overly protected children are less likely to cope with failure as they mature and the consequences become more severe.

Accountability, integrity, responsibility, and moral development are important life skills, but the development of these characteristics in young children often proves elusive. In an earlier era, American children had a very important part in family life and learned life skills as the family worked together. Children were vital to the success of the family structure, and they were considered a valuable asset. Today, it is common to see children and adolescents receiving from the family but often giving very little in return. Children are learning to run away from responsibility instead of embracing it.

"My neighbor went skiing last weekend and had a terrible accident. She was hit by a snow boarder and was knocked to the ground, breaking her arm and shoulder. The young man took off quickly and left her to fend for herself. The real tragedy is not that my neighbor was injured, because accidents do happen, but that this young adult lacked the moral consciousness to take responsibility for his actions and help someone in need.

Many children today are lacking accountability and moral character. My children are learning to be accountable for their choices and consequences through the Accountable Kids program. I am not trying to raise perfect children, but I hope to provide a solid foundation with opportunities to make good choices. The AK program is a back to basics approach that really works." S.W.

Values, Integrity, and Morals

The *AK* program teaches parents to instill positive character traits by using the traditional beliefs, work ethics, and values of our forefathers. Abigail Adams, wife of the second U.S. president, John

Adams, wrote to her son, "Great learning and superior abilities, should you ever possess them, will be of little value and small estimation, unless virtue, honor, truth, and integrity are added to them" (Bennett, 1998).

The purpose of the *AK* program is not only to teach children accountability and responsibility, but also to help them develop the values, integrity, and morals upon which our country was founded. Throughout the program, parents are presented with opportunities to teach and encourage children to develop the moral values that go hand in hand with accountability. The *AK* program uses the life lessons of completing chores, earning privileges, displaying positive behaviors, and working for future rewards to develop positive character traits.

Do incentives really work?

Incentives are a key part of the *Accountable Kids* program, but do they really work? Yes! Incentives are important to motivate children to begin a new behavior, but continuous incentives are not required to sustain the behavior. Immediate and continuous incentives are only used until the new, positive behavior becomes habitual. At this point, the behavior can be sustained

and strengthened by *intermittent* or irregular reinforcement. Webster's Dictionary defines intermittent as, "stopping and starting at intervals; pausing from time to time; periodic" (Macmillan, 1996). Reinforcements in the *AK* program are used sparingly and intermittently to produce long-term benefits after positive habits are developed.

The *AK* program does not encourage a reward system that teaches children to grow up expecting something for every action. Instead, children learn that rewards come at different times and in different ways. The final goal is for children to discover that some of the most important rewards come from within. The best measure of the success of the *AK* program is when children or adolescents get to the point where the outward framework of the program is no longer needed and children gain an internal sense of accountability that motivates their actions.

Ready to Go

Children can begin using the entire *Accountable Kids* program as soon as they understand the concept of choices and consequences. Generally this occurs between the ages of three and five, but there are aspects of the program that will work for younger children as well. The basic program does not change as the child matures and can be used well into the teenage years.

Initially the program will require planning, time, and dedication to implement, but the benefits are worth the effort. By fully embracing the *AK* program, parents and children will gain rewards that will last a lifetime.

The *Accountable Kids* book is complimented by an *Accountable Kids* Kit that includes everything necessary to begin teaching accountability today. The package includes an *Accountable Kids* Progress Board,

Responsibility Reminder Cards, Best Behavior Cards, Privilege Passes, Special Date Cards, and Bonus Bucks.

One Step at a Time

*" The greatest reward is not what we
receive for our labor,
but what we become by it."*
John Ruskin

Welcome to the *Accountable Kids (AK)* program.
The *AK* principles are not new, but the information is
gathered, organized, and implemented in a unique,
ready to use program. The concepts are simple and
build upon one another in an effective, structured
manner. The *AK* program is designed to help you
implement accountability using external tools and
principles backed by psychologists, educators, and
successful parents.

Four-Step Program

The Accountable Kids program is divided into four basic steps. Each step introduces new concepts and tools to help parents take accountability to the next level. It is helpful to understand one step before continuing on to the next. Each step may take one week, or several months, depending on the age and maturity of the child.

Parents are advised to follow *all* four steps outlined in the program. Allow the child to adapt to the new changes and benefit from the original program before deciding if certain parts are not working. Many of the long-term benefits can be seen only *after* children understand and test the program.

Step

Core Chores, Reminder Cards, Tickets, Best Behavior Cards, and a discipline program are introduced. These components help children gain a basic understanding of choices and consequences. Children learn to complete simple tasks without constant direction and begin to understand the difference between privileges and rights. They learn to budget time and resources. Parents gain knowledge of effective ways to discipline without losing control or using physical contact. Parents encourage children in a manner that sustains positive behaviors and values.

Step

The Privilege Pass and the Special Date Card is introduced. Parents gain an effective way to eliminate specific negative behaviors. Children learn to predict consequences, follow rules, and redirect themselves to positive behaviors. The importance of completing all of the Core Chores is reinforced and children begin to work toward future rewards. Children learn to plan and enjoy fun and positive interactions with a parent. The parent/child relationship is strengthened by spending quality time together.

Step

Extra Chores, Bonus Bucks, Savings, and helping others are introduced. Children learn that extra chores can be fun and rewarding. They begin to manage resources and establish self-imposed boundaries. They experience the advantages of saving and learn to budget and delay gratification. Parents have the opportunity to teach their children the difference between working for pay and helping others as service.

Step

The Family Forum and Quiet Time are introduced. The family learns productive ways to discuss goals, accomplishments, problems, and challenges. Children are taught lessons necessary for independent living. Children and parents experience the rewards of setting aside time to refresh and recharge themselves. Parents and children develop appropriate ways to manage stress and relax in positive ways.

Accountable Kids Components

The *AK* program introduces components in a specific order that encourages children to display desirable behaviors with various positive reinforcements such as Tickets, Bonus Bucks, Best Behavior Cards, Special Date Cards, and Privilege Passes. These positive reinforcements are external means to teach internal lessons. Each component targets specific areas helping children embrace accountability one step at a time.

Step 1 Components

The *AK* Progress Board

The *Accountable Kids* Progress Board becomes the central part of the *AK* program by providing a place to mark achievements and view goals. It serves as an individual progress chart. Children are encouraged to customize their board by painting, staining, or adding fun accessories.

Responsibility Reminder Cards

Responsibility Reminder Cards help children start and finish chores without parents having to direct every action. Children develop initiative and experience satisfaction from completing chores. The cards provide structure and predictability throughout the day because children know exactly what is required. They learn to become accountable for choices and consequences.

Parents are free to simply monitor progress and celebrate accomplishments.

Pets

Completing chores develops work ethics and positive habits. This helps children feel they are contributing members of the home. Reminder Cards help parents teach order, time management, and responsibility. Less time is spent directing children, and resources are used more effectively, creating more time for productive and fun activities.

The Reminder Cards effectively indicate what chores are to be completed and when they should be accomplished. The cards are flexible enough to grow with children as they progress from basic responsibilities to more complex jobs. For a complete list of all of the Reminder Cards and possible uses refer to Appendix B.

Appendix

Accountable Kids Tickets

Tickets are earned by completing basic chores. They are immediate reinforcements that can be exchanged for basic privileges and activities. Tickets empower children to make decisions about how they spend their free time throughout the day. The consistent use of Tickets extinguishes *entitlement,* because privileges are earned instead of simply given.

Ticket

Parents do not provide anything *extra* in the *AK* program. The privileges children earn are the same ones that parents have been previously giving. Tickets are effective tools in limiting activities such as television, computer time, video games, phone calls, movies, etc.

Disciplining with Tickets

For discipline to be effective, it must be immediate, consistent, and impact the child. Taking earned Tickets away provides a way for parents to discipline a child without losing control or using physical contact. Once a child experiences the value of Tickets, they can be taken away when a negative behavior is displayed. Effective discipline works when a child learns that negative behaviors result in negative consequences and positive behaviors result in positive consequences. A major goal of the *AK* program is to change the child's idea of discipline into self-discipline.

Real learning occurs when a child sees and experiences the relationship between action and consequences. Taking Tickets in a consistent and firm manner every time a negative behavior is exhibited can eliminate negative behaviors. This type of discipline will work quickly and effectively if a child values Tickets. A child learns that negative behaviors impact his ability to enjoy privileges. This type of discipline closely models real life consequences that adults encounter.

Best Behavior Card

The Best Behavior Card is used to foster and cultivate a specific positive behavior or value that is targeted by the parent. These cards also help sustain previously learned positive values and behaviors. The Best Behavior Card is an intermittent or periodic reinforcement. It is given occasionally to recognize and encourage positive behaviors. Children do not directly work for this card. The Best Behavior card can be used to motivate children to embrace concepts such as integrity, honesty, compassion, respect, and perseverance.

Best Behavior Card

The Best Behavior Card allows parents to acknowledge positive events such as helping others, speaking kindly, and performing acts of service. Each time a child receives a Best Behavior Card, it opens the door for communication and thought provoking comments that can lead to enhanced relationships, moral development, and internal reflection. The long-range goal of this component is to help children internalize values and virtues and gain an individual sense of identity. This establishes a basis for developing purpose and direction in life. Children can use an earned Best Behavior Card as a Ticket to enjoy privileges and activities, or parents can create a special weekly drawing using these cards.

Step  Components

Privilege Pass

The Privilege Pass helps eliminate a specific, negative behavior. It has been designed to empower children to predict consequences, follow rules, and redirect themselves toward positive behaviors. The Privilege Pass can motivate a child to go to bed without problems, complete homework on time, improve poor behavior at the dinner table, keep a

room clean, get up without reminders, improve manners and language, or complete a required task.

The Privilege Pass is earned when the child replaces a predetermined negative behavior with a specified positive behavior. Children have the option of using the Privilege Pass as a regular Ticket, but typically it is used to enjoy a special privilege or activity.

Special Date Card

The Special Date Card helps children to work for *future* rewards. Each day a sticker can be earned for the Special Date Card by completing all of the Core Chores. Children earn a special date when all ten boxes on the Special Date Card are filled with stickers. By consistently using this portion of the program, children learn to work for delayed rewards and discover they are capable of setting goals and reaching them. Relationships between children and parents are strengthened and enriched by spending positive and focused time together.

Step 3 Components

Bonus Bucks

The *Accountable Kids* program teaches children that every member of the home has responsibilities that need to be completed in order to enjoy the benefits of family life. Completing Core Chores provides basic privileges within the home, but it does not buy treats, toys, games, or activities that require money. While children earn Tickets by completing Core Chores, they can earn Bonus Bucks for completing Extra Chores. Bonus Bucks can be used as money for younger children, or can be traded in for real money once a week.

Extra Chores provide children the opportunity to  make money by going the extra mile. Paying children for Extra Chores is not designed to offer excessive amounts of spending money, but rather to provide an avenue for children to begin paying for more personal expenses. The more children earn, the more they become responsible for personal expenses and saving for the future.

Bonus Bucks provide an excellent opportunity to teach the benefits and principles of saving. Bonus Bucks encourage children to earn the things they want and release parents from the responsibility of having to provide everything. Children have the opportunity to weigh options and make decisions. Bonus Bucks provide children with a feeling of empowerment, self-confidence, and independence. As they gain more Bonus Bucks, children experience opportunity for saving, budgeting, delaying instant gratification, and working for future rewards.

Step  Components

Family Forum

The Family Forum is a key element in maintaining the *Accountable Kids* program with strength and fortitude. Parents can create structure and harmony within the home and turn problems into learning opportunities by consistently holding a regular family meeting.

The Family Forum is the time when parents and children meet together in an organized and focused manner to celebrate victories, coordinate schedules, set budgets, solve problems, disperse earnings, make new commitments, and unite together as a family. It establishes positive lines of communication between parents and children. This process helps children feel they are an integral part of the family and enables them to learn life skills necessary for independent living.

Quiet Time

Quiet Time is valuable for both parents and children. This experience is encouraged daily to allow the mind and body to regroup, refresh, and recharge. Quiet Time encourages imagination, productive behaviors, self-discipline, and self-entertainment. It is an opportunity to refocus and direct one's self in positive avenues.

Quiet Time encourages parents and children to find productive ways to relax. It establishes an opportunity to manage stress and pursue areas of interest. This time provides a buffer for the physical and emotional demands of both growing up and parenting.

The Accountable Kids Program Develops:

- ➤ Accountability
- ➤ Responsibility
- ➤ Respect
- ➤ Integrity
- ➤ Self-empowerment
- ➤ Self-discipline
- ➤ Confidence
- ➤ Emotional awareness
- ➤ Internal motivation
- ➤ Moral values
- ➤ Initiative
- ➤ Work ethics
- ➤ Ability to predict consequences

Step Forward with Knowledge

It is helpful to gain a basic understanding of a child's psychological development before implementing the *Accountable Kids* program. This chapter discusses different theories, beliefs, and experiments relating to child development and presents how children reason, behave, and learn. This information allows parents to see where children are developmentally and specifically tailor the program to match their individual needs. The *AK* program helps parents focus on age appropriate values and behaviors that are developmentally appropriate for each child.

How Your Child Thinks

Many people consider Jean Piaget to be one of the greatest developmental psychologists of our time. Piaget's work was based on two major concepts:

➢ Children learn by themselves and are not simply taught by adults.
➢ Children think entirely differently from adults - they do not merely know less.

Piaget developed a comprehensive and compelling theory of cognitive development that is of tremendous importance in understanding how children think and behave. He divided children into four groups:

➢ Sensory-motor Intelligence
➢ Preoperational Thought
➢ Operational Thought
➢ Formal Operational Thought

Sensory-motor Intelligence (Birth to 2 years)

The young child begins to organize physical actions such as sucking, grasping, hitting, and walking to deal with the immediate world. There are different stages during this time that take a baby from simple reflexes to the beginnings of thought.

The Preoperational Child (2 to 6 years)

The preoperational child undergoes great changes. The child's mind rapidly advances to understand images and words. Thinking is *unsystematic and illogical*. This is a time of great imagination and wonderment, a time to believe in Santa Claus, the Tooth Fairy, and the Easter Bunny. The child lives in the *here and now* and views the world from his/her perspective only. The preoperational child is learning to cooperate with other children, but predominately plays along side other children. Children in this stage are unable to think through a situation and then reverse the situation. Perception is stronger than logic at this age.

HELPFUL HINT: The preoperational child may be confused when parents attempt to reason or ask questions that require thinking back to an original situation. It is helpful to keep all questions and lessons short and simple with children in this stage. Less is often more.

A preoperational child is considered to be *egocentric*. This does not mean the child is selfish, but merely unable to distinguish her perspective from another's and believes that her interests are the same as others. Piaget demonstrated this by taking a child on a walk around a model of three mountains. The child sat on one side of a table and a doll was placed opposite the child facing a different view of the mountains. The preoperational child could pick the picture that represented her own view of the mountains, but was unable to pick the card that represented the doll's view. The preoperational child was unable to determine that the doll had a different perspective. The older, operational child could pick the card that represented her viewpoint and also the doll's perspective (Crain, 1980).

> **HELPFUL HINT:** Preoperational children assume their wants are the same as everyone else's. They don't realize that others might have a different viewpoint. Parents can encourage sharing and cooperation with children in this stage, but these skills are not fully understood until about age six.

The Operational Child (7 to 11 years)

The operational child is able to think logically and systematically when dealing with concrete ideas and activities. His world is more stable and thinking becomes organized. He is able to observe something and reverse the situation to come up with a logically produced answer. He can see another person's perspective and recognize that other people have different interests and tastes. The operational child plays *with* other children in *joint* endeavors.

Formal Operational (11 to adulthood)

At this stage a child's thought process expands to abstract and hypothetical thinking and reasoning. She can organize thoughts mentally and possesses the ability to understand hypothetical possibilities. A child in this stage may solve problems scientifically by testing different possibilities and trying out various combinations. A formal operational child considers all options, and the thinking process reaches a new level.

This new thought process can lead to idealism and ideas of a better world. The child now understands abstract concepts such as liberty, justice, and love. (It is interesting to note that most adults do not use formal operational thinking consistently, but rather only in the areas of their interest.)

Fun Experiments

Fun experiments are included to help you determine the developmental stage of your child. It is important to understand how your child thinks and reasons before starting the *AK* program. The following experiments will provide insight into how your child perceives the world and solves problems. The experiments are not to be used to teach your child the correct answer, but rather they are an opportunity to observe how your child thinks, reasons, and perceives life.

Experiment #1

Place pennies on a table and create two equal rows with the pennies moderately spaced. Ask your child if one row has more pennies or if the rows are the same. He will probably agree that the two rows are the same.

Now, compact one row of pennies as your child watches, so that one row is shorter. Ask your child if one row has more pennies in it. The preoperational child will believe that the longer row has more pennies in it, even though you have not added or taken any pennies away. The operational child may go back and forth between the rows, but will decide that the two rows still have the same number of pennies.

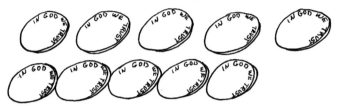

Experiment #2

Place two clear glasses with equal amounts of water in front of your child. Ask which glass has more water. Your child will probably state that both glasses have the same amount of  water. While your child watches, pour the water from one of the glasses into a wider glass. Ask which glass now has more water. Do not respond in any way or tell your child if he is right or wrong, simply observe his perceptions.

The preoperational child will say that the glass with the highest level of water contains more liquid. This child cannot understand that the water amount is the same, because nothing has been added or taken away. The child at this developmental stage is more influenced by perception than logic. The child in the operational stage of development will be able to discern that the two amounts of liquid are still identical, because nothing has been added or lost.

Experiment #3

Hold two equal balls of clay and ask your child if they are the same size. She will probably agree the two balls of clay are the same size.

Take one ball and roll it into a long rope shape while your child watches. Now, ask which one has more clay. The preoperational child believes that the clay rope is larger because it is longer. Even though your child watched you roll the clay into a rope and saw you did not add or take anything away, the preoperational child cannot reverse her thinking to realize nothing has changed but the shape.

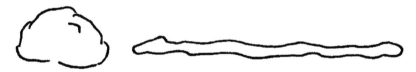

The preoperational child can only focus on one aspect of a problem and cannot consider two dimensions of a situation at the same time. The older, operational child will consider that nothing has changed in the amount of clay, so the two are still equal.

Experiment #4

Draw lines on six index cards. Have the lines represent a stick standing up and then falling down. The first card would have a straight vertical line and the last would be a straight horizontal line. The four other cards would have lines somewhere in-between. As your child observes, take a pencil and hold it upright. Let the pencil fall down to the ground. Show your child the cards and have him put the cards in the order of the pencil standing up to falling down. Sometimes the preoperational child will get the first and last cards right, but usually will not be able to place the remaining cards in order.

The preoperational child has difficulty seeing transformation or depicting an action sequence. Although this progression is obvious to an adult, the preoperational child does not see the action sequence because he sees the drawings as a series of different states and not a whole picture. It is as though the child views life as a series of pictures instead of an entire movie. The operational child will see the entire sequence and place the cards in the correct order (Crain, 1980).

Following Rules

Lawrence Kohlberg expanded on Piaget's work by focusing on moral development. He was not interested in a child's immediate answer to a dilemma, but the *reasoning* behind the answer. The following story is commonly used to determine the moral judgment of children.

Heinz Steals Medicine

A woman in Europe was dying from cancer. The doctors believed she might be saved if she received a medicine that contained radium. The medicine could be made for $200, but the pharmacist charged $2,000 for the drug. The woman's husband worked very hard to raise the money to buy the medicine, but he could only raise one half of the price.

The man pleaded with the pharmacist to let him buy the medicine with the money he had. The pharmacist would not sell the drug for any less. The husband loved his wife very much, and in desperation he broke into the pharmacy at night and stole the drug to save his wife's life (Kohlberg, 1963).

Read this story to your child and ask if the man's actions were right. Then, ask your child what the man's consequence should be. By listening to your child's answers, you will learn how your child views rules and moral dilemmas.

The preoperational child will perceive that all rules are fixed and cannot be changed because they come from a higher authority. He will probably say the man should not have stolen the medicine and should be punished. The operational child will weigh the actions of the man. Although the child may believe stealing is wrong, he may justify the action because the man was trying to save his wife's life.

HELPFUL HINT: An operational child may disobey or argue if he feels rules are unfair, but a preoperational child often will not question rules.

Preoperational Child (Ages 2 to 6)
> Cannot reverse logical situations
> Cannot see things from another's perspective
> Believes rules are absolute
> Has difficulty understanding time
> Thinks unsystematically and illogically
> Considers only one dimension of a problem at a time

Operational Child (Ages 7 to 11)
> Considers two aspects of a problem at one time
> Sees things from another person's perspective
> Believes rules can be changed if unfair
> Thinks logically and systematically when dealing with concrete objects and activities

Formal Operational Child (Age 11 to Adulthood)
> Thinking is abstract and hypothetical
> Orders thoughts mentally
> Reasons scientifically
> Considers all possibilities

Stages of Development

Erik Erikson had a dramatic effect on the psychoanalytic theory of development. Erickson believed that as children progressed through stages of development, they would experience both positive and negative attributes, or characteristics, in each stage. The desired outcome was that children would experience a higher ratio of positive attributes so they would not carry a *deficit* to the next stage.

The *AK* program teaches parents to recognize important stages in their children's lives. By recognizing the stages of development, parents can encourage growth at appropriate times and maintain appropriate expectations about their children's abilities. If children do not successfully master a developmental stage, it may prove more difficult later in life.

The *AK* program teaches parents that positive attributes can be learned through conscious decisions, hard work, and proper use of parenting tools.

Developmental Stages
1. *Trust vs. Mistrust - (Birth to 1 year)*
The child learns to coordinate body movements and discovers that objects exist out of his sight. Confidence, drive, and hope are attributed to the child experiencing more trust than mistrust.

2. *Autonomy vs. Shame and Doubt - (1 to 2 years)*
The child is exploring choices and exercising his will. She wants to do things on her own, but is becoming aware of social expectations and pressures. She is becoming self-conscious about how others see her and view her mistakes. Erickson believed that a child develops *self-determination* in this stage if she does not experience lasting feelings of shame and doubt.

Sally's parents were working to toilet train her. One day at the store the little girl had an accident, and her parents were faced with a difficult mess. In their frustration and embarrassment, they scolded Sally. She looked around and saw strangers looking at her and felt shamed.

The next day her parents were surprised to see Sally wouldn't use the bathroom. She had developed doubt in her abilities and felt embarrassed and shamed by the experience.

3. Initiative vs. Guilt - (3 to 6 years)

A child in this stage is often daring, competitive, and curious. She is eager to learn, imaginative, and full of ambition. Unfortunately as she makes mistakes and is reprimanded for taking the initiative, she feels guilty and suppressed. The child begins to learn that some of her dreams and plans are too dangerous, messy, or unattainable, so she learns to keep her impulses in check in order to avoid failure and reprimands. She then feels guilty that she is unable to fulfill her parent's hopes and dreams. If a child does not experience lasting feelings of guilt, *direction* and *purpose* will be developed during this stage.

Megan is four and wants to do everything by herself. One day she decided to make peanut butter sandwiches. She got out the bread and smeared the peanut butter and jam on the sandwiches.

Megan and her sister were proudly eating when her mom walked into the kitchen.

Megan's mom was upset to see peanut butter and jam everywhere. She got mad at Megan for making a mess. She told Megan that in the future she was not allowed to get out food without permission.

Before her mom came in, Megan felt proud about her accomplishment, but afterward she felt <u>guilty</u>, believing she had done something wrong.

The next time Megan thinks about trying something on her own, she may doubt her abilities and decide she shouldn't take the <u>initiative</u>. Megan's mom overlooked the positive side of her daughter attempting to do something on her own and only saw the mess.

Christine's five-year-old boy, Dylan, is in Erickson's <u>initiative</u> stage of development. He wanted to help clean the house, so he got window cleaner and proceeded to spray and wipe everything he could see. After various items in the house were dripping wet and smeared with a towel, he moved outside to clean the sliding glass door.

Christine found Dylan outside in the freezing cold, cleaning the glass door. The window cleaner was freezing onto the glass, and Dylan was smearing the icy  *mess everywhere. In spite of this, he was proud of himself. He had taken the initiative and felt he was helping. Because Christine was aware of the developmental stage Dylan was in, she realized the importance of allowing him to take the initiative.*

Christine thanked Dylan for helping, but then allowed him to be accountable for his actions by showing him how to clean the windows. She then helped him finish the job correctly, modeling the appropriate actions.

4. *Industry vs. inferiority - (6 to 11 years)*

The child in this stage moves from hopes and wishes and begins to learn new skills. He wants to feel competent, useful, and skillful. If a child does not experience lasting feelings of inferiority, *competency* and *individual skills* are developed in this stage.

> *John lives in a fast-paced home where both parents work. A woman comes in to clean the home, and dinner is usually take-out or prepared quickly. When John attempts to help his mother, she gets frustrated because he takes too long. His mother feels she can do things better and faster.*
>
> *John begins to feel unneeded and incapable of helping. He feels inferior to his parents and believes his efforts are not valuable. John does not have chores to do and does not develop work skills.*
>
> *Later in life, John's parents wonder why John (the adult) does not possess work ethics, is not driven, has few skills, and is not industrious. They are baffled because they work hard and can't understand why John does not seem able to accept adult responsibilities.*

5. *Identity vs. Role Confusion - (11 to 18 years)*

This can be a turbulent and uncertain time for children. Physical changes and social pressures are experienced. Children begin to think hypothetically and entertain limitless possibilities concerning who they are and what they will become. If they do not become committed to their *own* values, beliefs, religious convictions, and goals, they may become confused and lack a sense of identity and purpose.

It is common for children at this age to push away from the family system in an attempt to test different ideas and values. This can be a difficult time for parents because children are testing boundaries, severing ties, and breaking rules. Understanding this process can help parents remain calm when children begin to think differently and experiment with new ideas and concepts.

This does not mean that family rules and values can be disregarded. Children want to make their own choices, but parents can still expect them to abide by family rules and experience pre-established consequences. Children have the right to their own personal beliefs, but parents also have the right to protect the moral standards within the home. Modeling appropriate positive behaviors is very important in this stage.

HELPFUL HINT: Knowing the developmental abilities of your child will help you encourage appropriate age related skills.

How Children Learn

John Locke was one of the early theorists in psychology. He concluded that thoughts and feelings are derived through a process of learning by association, imitation, rewards, punishments, and repetition. Understanding Locke's process of learning reinforces the basic principles of the *Accountable Kids* program. A child first learns how to clean his room by *watching*. He *imitates* how his mother hangs and folds his clothes. As he receives *positive rewards* for these behaviors, he continues to clean his room over and over again until he develops the habit from *repeated behavior* (Locke, 1963).

> **Association** – When a child regularly observes two ideas at the same time, he begins to *associate* them together. If a child had a positive or negative experience in a particular place, that feeling may come back automatically if he is returned to the same environment.

> **Imitation** – A child loves to *imitate* the people around him. If a parent yells and screams, it is easy to see why a child grows up imitating this behavior. A child will imitate good and bad behaviors. When a child sees a parent acting responsible and accountable, she is more likely to value and imitate these activities. Modeling positive behaviors is very important. It can be helpful to do "chores" alongside a child such as brush teeth together, help with the dishes, or take out the trash with each other.

> **Reward and Punishment** – A child will continue to do activities that bring encouragement and *positive rewards* and eliminate activities that deliver *punishments* and negative consequences. Rewards and punishments can be deceiving. Parents may consider certain discipline measures as punishment, but if a child continues to display a behavior over and over, it is because he is receiving some sort of reward for this behavior. A child may consider the "punishment" a reward,

because it brings attention from the parent. Unfortunately, negative attention is sometimes better than no attention at all.

➢ **Repetition** – A child who performs an activity or behavior *repeatedly* will develop the habit and continue the behavior without prompting or external incentives. Hopefully, as a positive behavior is repeatedly executed, the internal satisfaction will be internalized and maintained.

"This week we had a major breakthrough. We have been consistently using the Accountable Kids program in our home for two months. My oldest daughter took to the program right away and has been doing great. It has been fun and exciting to see her become accountable for her actions. I am relieved to stop dictating her every move.

Unfortunately, my four-year old son had limited success with the program until this week. He just couldn't grasp the idea that Tickets would allow him to enjoy activities and Bonus Bucks would buy things. We were consistent and offered opportunities for our son to understand the program using Locke's process of learning. We provided opportunities for our son to associate the benefits of Tickets and Bonus Bucks. He watched his sister use her Tickets and Bonus Bucks to buy privileges and store bought items. He experienced positive and negative consequences. We were consistent with the program hoping he would begin to understand the correlation between choices and consequences.

Last week we were at the store and my son saw something he really wanted. He turned to me and asked if he had enough Bonus Bucks to buy the toy. He finally got it! He had earned enough money to purchase something he wanted and experienced the rewards of his earnings. After that day, he took off with the program. He now moves his Reminder Cards on his own, and I do not have to direct him to do his responsibilities. He is now working for a new toy and is even motivated to do Extra Chores. I was beginning to think that this program was just not for him, but finally he understood he had the power to manage his own life." A.H.

Shaping Behavior

Not only can a child's behavior be shaped, but the frequency of the behavior can also be influenced. B.F. Skinner, a pioneer in behavioral psychology, expanded on Ivan Pavlov's Classic Conditioning Theory and was the heir to John Locke's work. Skinner demonstrated that behaviors could be shaped and the frequency increased by using *intermittent*, or irregular, reinforcement.

Skinner trained a pigeon to push a bar that released a food pellet by shaping the desired behavior step by step. At first the pigeon was rewarded when it looked in the direction of the bar. Then the bird only received

food if it moved toward the bar. The expectations were increased until the bird only received food when it pecked at the bar. The bird was encouraged to perform a specific behavior using an immediate reward. After the bird learned the desired behavior, the pigeon only received the reward from time to time, or *intermittently*, which reinforced the behavior for a longer period of time.

Skinner tried a variety of experiments to determine which pattern of reinforcement would yield the most pecks by the pigeon. His results indicated that intermittent reinforcement produced the highest yield and sustained the behavior for the longest period of time after the reinforcement was completely withdrawn (Crain, 1980).

In essence, this is the same theory upon which large casinos are built. When a person gambles, he never knows when the payoff will come. He continues to put money in the machine, hopeful he will be rewarded on the next pull.

> **HELPFUL HINT:** Behaviors are shaped by reinforcement. It is possible to encourage negative or positive behaviors. If a child continues to display a negative behavior, he is likely receiving some type of reward for that behavior.

Encouraging Positive Behaviors

The *Accountable Kids* program begins by recognizing, encouraging, and rewarding positive behaviors. B. F. Skinner concluded, "If we wish to begin a desirable form of behavior, it is usually best to begin with continuous reinforcement; this is the most efficient way to get the behavior started. However, if we also wish to make the behavior last, we might at some point switch to an intermittent schedule" (Bijou and Baer, 1961, p. 62).

As a child progresses in the *AK* program, parents are encouraged to withdraw direct involvement and allow the program to run with minimal effort, encouragement, and prompting. Children learn they are not rewarded for every action, but continue to progress and develop inner motivation and self-discipline. Specific tools in the AK program have been incorporated to help parents establish positive behaviors and then sustain these behaviors. The Privilege Pass is an immediate reward. Children earn this card every time a specific positive behavior is displayed. This type of reinforcement establishes the positive behavior. After the positive behavior becomes habitual, parents can transition to the Best Behavior Card, which is an intermittent reinforcement, to sustain positive behaviors.

Eventually, the tools used in the *AK* program are replaced with contracts and verbal arrangements. Once children experience the joy and power of true accountability and self-reliance, these feelings become the basic motivators and are hopefully solidified as personal values.

Eliminating Negative Behaviors

It is very difficult to extinguish undesirable behaviors such as begging, arguing, whining, and temper tantrums that have been reinforced intermittently. A child will persist in the negative behavior, thinking that at some point the payoff will come. Just like gambling in a casino, a child continues the negative behavior, believing it will produce a reward eventually.

HELPFUL HINT: If you give in to your child (even once) when he complains or argues, you are encouraging this behavior in the future.

Extinguishing undesirable behaviors requires consistency. Your child must experience consistent consequences to eliminate a specific negative behavior. Even after a positive behavior is established, your child may attempt to test the boundaries from time to time to see if the consequences remain.

Applying Knowledge

It is beneficial to determine a child's developmental stage so parents can individually tailor the *AK* program to that child's moral, cognitive, emotional, and developmental level. While the *AK* program is designed to be functional for a variety of children, parents may want to promote values that reflect their child's stage of development. Parents may also want to focus their energy, and their child's energy, on a particular concept in the program that teaches the developmental skills appropriate to that age level.

The *AK* program helps children progress in their reasoning and logical thinking. Children experience choice and consequence, but they understand it on different levels for different ages. The following developmental charts describe the advantages of each component used in the *AK* program. Each component can be specifically targeted to promote appropriate values and behaviors for each developmental stage. Parents can use this information to focus on the current developmental stage of a child. This enables parents to look ahead to see how the child will transition into the next stage.

HELPFUL HINT: The thought process of young children is very different from adults. The *AK* program will be more successful if it is structured to a child's developmental stage.

Preoperational (ages 2-6)

The key developmental tasks for children at this stage center around the development of *initiative and autonomy*. It is helpful to keep discussions short and to the point. Children at this stage are just beginning to develop the capacity to consider another person's perspective. They live in the *here and now* and have difficulty managing time. A preoperational child is learning good and bad, true and false, and right and wrong. At this stage it is difficult to distinguish fantasy from reality. Perspective is stronger than logic.

How AK Benefits Preoperational Child

Chore Cards	Provide structure to a child's day • promote independence as a child begins to learn about responsibilities and work • encourage a child to start a chore • help parents focus on initiative instead of quality of work
Tickets	Help a child gain some control over the day • provide parents with effective discipline without losing control • reinforce the difference between right and wrong and promote a basic understanding of choices and consequences • effectively limit exposure to idle activities
Bonus Bucks	Provide an avenue to purchase items • direct a child toward completing extra jobs
Best Behavior Card	Encourages and reinforces good behavior and positive values
Privilege Pass	Targets positive behaviors and eliminates negative behaviors • encourages a child to focus on a specific positive behavior
Special Date Card	Encourages working for future rewards • helps a child feel special and loved by spending focused time with a parent
Family Forum	Establishes rules and consequences • reinforces concepts of right and wrong and promotes positive values • helps a child feel valued and considered
Quiet Time	Provides rest and promotes self-control • presents an opportunity to self-entertain

Operational (ages 7-11)

The key developmental tasks for children in this stage center around the development of *industry, skills, and work ethics*. Children are learning to think abstractly, so more details can be used in discussions. Children can reason logically and think through problems and solutions. Operational children begin to manage resources and comprehend a future time enabling them to predict short-term consequences.

How AK Benefits Operational Child

Chore Cards	Support the idea that work can be rewarding • reinforce work ethics and specific life skills • help child develop *quality* in his work
Tickets	Provide benefits for completing basic responsibilities • encourage child to budget time and resources
Bonus Bucks	Reinforce work ethics • encourage a child to successfully complete Extra Chores • help a child manage resources, appreciate monetary items and promote saving money for future purchases
Best Behavior Card	Encourages and sustains positive behaviors • acknowledges personal values and virtues
Privilege Pass	Reinforces positive choices and develops habits that carry into adulthood
Special Date Card	Encourages child to plan ahead and experience the results of delayed gratification • stresses the importance of completing all Core Chores • establishes a time for a parent and child to interact in fun and positive ways
Family Forum	Provides an opportunity for the child to voice opinions and be included in family decisions • creates an avenue to establish fair rules • reinforces the benefits of organization and cooperation
Quiet Time	Provides an opportunity to refocus and direct in a positive direction

Formal Operational (ages 11- adulthood)

The key developmental tasks for children in this stage center around the development of *personal identity*. Thinking becomes hypothetical, and a child can consider many possibilities to problems and solutions. Discussions can become deeper and more involved. The formal operational child is searching for true beliefs and internalizing principles as he becomes a unique individual. At this stage, the child can predict short and long term consequences.

How AK Benefits Formal Operational Child

Chore Cards	Develop self-esteem through accomplishment • provide basic reminders for completing basic chores • provide a transition into contracts and verbal agreements
Tickets	Reinforce the idea that privileges are earned and not given • help a child learn to prioritize responsibilities and privileges
Bonus Bucks	Help a child to manage financial resources • empower • help establish self-imposed boundaries
Best Behavior Card	Helps internalize values, empathy, and identity • encourages child to live life with purpose
Privilege Pass	Empowers a child to more appropriately use agency to achieve desired results • helps establish positive patterns to take into adulthood
Special Date Card	Fosters strong relationships with parents • provides opportunities to discuss sensitive concerns and issues
Family Forum	Helps a child learn lessons to live independently • teaches the family that resources are limited • develops organizational skills and planning
Quiet Time	Encourages a child to explore interests and find productive avenues to relax • establishes an avenue to manage stress and a time to search for identity and purpose

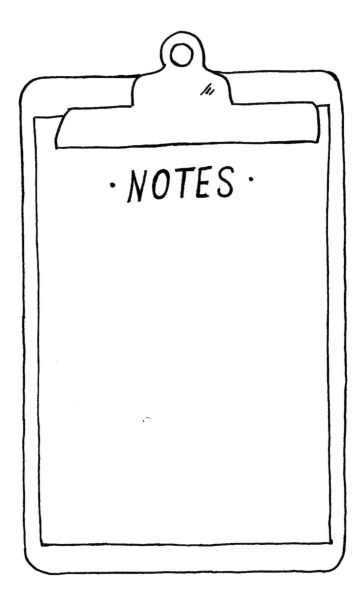

Starting the Accountable Kids Program

It's now time to put the *Accountable Kids* program into action! The *AK* program is divided into four steps. Your child progresses to the next step after the current concepts are learned and understood. Preoperational children may spend one week to one month learning the concepts in each step, where older children will typically be ready to progress in weekly intervals. If special circumstances prevail, you may remain at any step for an extended time period.

49

for Initial Preparation

1. Read and understand the *AK* program presented in Chapter One and determine your child's developmental stage presented in Chapter Three.

2. Prepare your cards.
   A. If you have more than one child, label the cards with a distinctive mark for each child to avoid confusion.
   B. The Accountable Kids cards are treated with a special coating for durability, but they can be laminated for additional protection.

3. Set up a system where your child can complete most chores independently. It is important for your child to experience the satisfaction of completing chores on his own.

> *"My five-year old daughter Meg was having trouble completing all of her chores without continual help. We made some simple changes that allowed Meg to complete most of her chores on her own. We purchased a pump toothpaste dispenser, stocked her vitamins in a weekly container, and helped her lay her clothes out before going to bed. The changes were very simple, and now Meg only needs help with her hair in the morning." S.W.*

4. Personalize the Progress Board. The boards can be painted, stained, decorated, and customized with your child's name.

5. Hang the Progress Board in a visible area. The board becomes the focal point of the *AK* program. The kitchen, hallway, and living room are all great locations. It is important that both you and your child see the board throughout the day. If the board is not easily seen, it is easily forgotten.

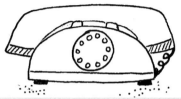

We received a call from a mother who couldn't get her son to use the Accountable Kids program on a daily basis. He couldn't remember to hang up his Reminder Cards and was not completing all of his responsibilities. His board had been placed on the back of his bedroom door so younger siblings wouldn't bother it. Because it was out of sight, it was out of mind. When the board was moved to the kitchen, the difference was dramatic. He used the board throughout the day, and he and his mother became aware of his progress and achievements.

6. Meet with your child to discuss the *AK* program. Be very specific about what will occur during the first step.
    A. Discuss the benefits and rewards your child will experience.
    B. Let your child know this is a program designed to empower him and give him control over his life.

"My husband and I both read the AK book and learned the details of the program. We called a family meeting and introduced the program to our family. Each child was given a Progress Board, and we discussed different options for individualizing them. We planned a night to paint and stain the boards. We

discussed the individual benefits of implementing the program and pointed out the ways it would help the entire family. We established rules for Ticketed Activities and Core Chores, and set up guidelines for losing Tickets. We selected a date to begin using the AK program.

The first week was amazing. There was an immediate change in our home. My children began taking responsibility for their own personal chores, and I no longer directed every move. I was able to recognize positive actions with Best Behavior Cards and stop negative behaviors by taking Tickets away. I saw my children rationing their time with television and video games, which is something they never did. We set up clear rules for chores, Ticketed Activities, and discipline measures, and placed pictures and lists on the fridge as a reminder.

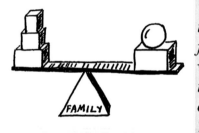

We met again in a week to discuss our progress as a family. We saw the program was helping our family use time better, giving us more opportunity to do fun things. That night we presented Step Two of the program. During the first part of week two we experienced the 'testing time'. The children pushed the limits many times, and Tickets were lost. The children were testing our resolve, seeing if we were really going to hold true to our established consequences.

That week was a turning point for our family. My children finally realized that actions equaled consequences. They learned that the rules we set up were going to be kept. By the end of the week, we were back on track. The AK program was making life easier, and my children were getting along better.

Each week we continued to introduce another step until we had incorporated the entire program. It was easy for our family to learn the concepts one step at a time. Our children are now responsible for running the program and are accountable for their decisions.

Their jobs either get an approval or a 'do again'. They have learned to complete a job correctly the first time, because it is so much faster and easier. I am no longer the one prodding them along to complete tasks. This has been an answer to our prayers. Thank You!!!"
S.A.

Selecting Chores

The *Accountable Kids* kit includes over fifty Reminder Cards showing the most common chores for children. Step One of the *AK* program helps your child learn that completing basic responsibilities earns basic privileges.

Clean Room

 **to Selecting Chores**

1. Go through the Reminder Cards and divide the cards into two piles: Core Chores and Extra Chores.
   A. Core Chores are your child's basic responsibilities and are the bare minimum for living in your home. Core Chores are the tasks for which you are not willing to pay you child.
   B. Extra Chores are the jobs for which your child will receive compensation. Set the Extra Chores aside for now as they will be explained in Step Three of the

Appendix

program. (Refer to Appendix C for sample schedules for different ages and stages).

2. Review the Core Chores you have chosen for your child. Make certain these chores are all basic tasks you want accomplished every day.

3. Your child will be encouraged to perform *all* of the Core Chores every day. These chores are now officially your child's responsibility unless specifically excused.

   A. Keep the Core Chores simple so they can be completed in minimal time. Most Core Chores should be tasks your child is already performing such as getting dressed, brushing teeth, and making the bed.

   B. Don't overload your child with Core Chores. If there are too many Core Chores in the beginning, more time will be spent at the Progress Board attempting to figure out what to do, rather than developing positive habits.

4. The Reminder Cards remind your child to complete chores. If the card is misplaced, the chore is still required.

Sam told his mom his morning chores were completed. She noticed that his bed was not made and asked him to meet her at the AK board for a 'Chart Check'. Sam had completed all of the morning chores that were on the board, but the 'Make Bed' Reminder Card was missing. Sam told his mom he didn't need to make his bed because it was not on the AK Board. This was a job with which Sam was currently struggling.

This situation provided his mom with an opportunity to discuss the purpose of the Reminder Cards. Sam learned he had certain responsibilities every day and was responsible to make sure all of his chores were completed. The cards were simply used as a reminder.

Sam was responsible to make his bed every day. Since he had not completed all of his chores, he did not earn a Ticket for the morning chores, nor did he earn a sticker for the Date Card. His mom helped him make another Reminder Card and let him know that he was responsible for the care of his cards and board. She let him know that if he lost another Reminder Card, it would cost him a Ticket.

 ps for Selecting Chores

➢ Core Chores do not vary. They are your child's responsibility every day.
➢ Core Chores should be measurable and observable. Your child should know exactly what is expected.
➢ Keep these chores simple in the beginning.

Customizing Reminder Cards

The color bars on the Reminder Cards can be cut to represent a particular time of day the chore is to be completed. Your child will learn to accomplish chores at appropriate times by referring to the color bar on the bottom of the Reminder Card. By

completing chores at specific times, your child will learn order, time management, and responsibility.

Cutting the Reminder Cards is optional, however most parents find it simplifies the process by designating chores into specific time periods that are easily recognized.

 **for Using Reminder Cards**

1. The Reminder Cards should be divided into two categories: Core Chores and Extra Chores. The Core Chores can now be cut to represent the time of day the task is to be completed.

- A. Cut the <u>Morning</u> Reminder Cards, leaving only the <u>yellow</u> bar.
- B. Cut the <u>Day</u> Reminder Cards, leaving the <u>red</u> bar on the bottom.
- C. Cut the <u>Evening</u> Reminder Cards, leaving the <u>blue</u> bar on the bottom.
- D. Do not cut the Extra Chores for now.
- E. If you are unsure about the timing of a chore or do not know if you want the task to be a Core Chore, do not cut the card.

Clean Room

Clean Room

Clean Room

2. Hang the Reminder Cards for Core Cores on the Start Peg. Organize the cards so the Evening Chores (blue) are on the bottom, the Day Chores (red) next, and the Morning Chores (yellow) are on the top. This is the starting order for each day.

3. Present the Reminder Cards to your child. Show her how to distinguish the difference between Morning, Day, and Evening Chores by referring to the color bars.
   A. <u>Yellow</u> bars represent <u>Morning</u> Chores.
   B. <u>Red</u> bars represent <u>Day</u> Chores.
   C. <u>Blue</u> bars represent <u>Evening</u> Chores.
   D. <u>Purple</u> and <u>green</u> bars represent <u>Extra Chores</u>. Extra Chores will be presented in Step Three of the program.

It will become apparent why the Reminder Cards are cut as you use the program. Cutting the Reminder Cards to leave a particular color at the bottom makes it easy to know when a color grouping of chores is completed.

HELPFUL HINT: Privileges can be restricted until chores are completed to encourage children to manage resources.

4. Discuss the deadlines for Morning, Day, and Evening Chores with your child. Explain that when a chore is completed on time, the Reminder Card is hung on the Finish Peg. Let your child know that particular chores are appropriately completed in the morning (brush teeth, make bed), some are to be accomplished in the

afternoon (set dinner table, do homework), and some are properly completed in the evening (get ready for bed, feed pet, brush teeth). Make sure your child knows that it is not only important to complete a chore, but it is important to complete the chore at the *correct time*.

    A. If the group of chores is not completed before the established deadline, *no* credit is given for completing that particular set of chores. For example, if your child does not complete *all* of his Morning Chores before school, a Ticket is not earned for Morning Chores.

    B. Teach your child that chores can be completed in any order within a color grouping. For example, if your child's morning chores are brush teeth, make bed, and clean room, he can complete these chores in any order.

5. Discuss the requirements for fully completing each chore. Your child should know exactly what is expected for each chore to be considered finished. A Good Job form is provided so you can list the exact requirements for each job (Appendix E).

    A. It is helpful to work alongside your child in the beginning to demonstrate the requirements for completing each chore.

    B. You can monitor and evaluate your child's progress, but it is not your responsibility to prod or remind. Teach your child to complete chores, move Reminder Cards, and then report back to you.

    C. Establish incremental steps to continually improve the quality of your child's work.

    D. Once your child understands and is capable of completing chores, do not provide reminders. Allow your child to experience the results of his choices and then adjust his behavior to obtain desired results.

6. If your child is having difficulty finishing chores, try using a timer to teach him to work within a certain time frame.
   A. Place a timer in a spot where your child can see how much time he has to complete his chores.
   B. An option is to have your child earn an extra Ticket if his chores are completed before the timer goes off. Later, a spinner can be used to allow the child a chance to "spin" for an extra Ticket if the chores are completed before the timer goes off. This transitions your child from a continuous reward to an intermittent reinforcement.

Ashley was having difficulty cleaning the playroom. The room would get so messy that it became overwhelming to pick up. In frustration, her mother set a timer and told Ashley that any toys not put away after the timer rang would be thrown away or put in a box for her to earn back. In essence, Ashley would be punished for not being able to beat the timer.

As soon as the timer came out, Ashley would become upset and frantically try to pick up toys. She would usually get the playroom cleaned before the timer went off, but she would be unhappy and anxious during the entire cleaning process.

When Ashley's mom began the Accountable Kids program, she started <u>encouraging</u> Ashley's positive behavior, instead of <u>punishing</u> her for not achieving the desired result. Ashley was given a small incentive for beating the timer in the beginning. This established the positive behavior. Then the frequency of the reward was changed to sustain the behavior. If Ashley beat the timer, she could spin a small game wheel and try to win a Ticket.

Sometimes she would win a Ticket, but often she won nothing. The intermittent reward ingrained the habit of happily cleaning the playroom into Ashley's behavior. Ashley learned to clean the playroom in a timely manner and eventually did not expect a reward for completing her responsibility.

HELPFUL HINT: A positive incentive works much better than a negative one to motivate and sustain good behavior.

7. Your child's chores will be very simple and specific in the beginning. The idea is to establish the basic habit of completing chores and being responsible. As your child progresses in the program, you can require more by combining Reminder Cards to represent multiple activities. For example, your child may start out with "make bed" and "clean room" cards. After the two tasks become habitual, you can remove one card and redefine the remaining card to include both tasks. You can define the requirements using the *Reminder Card* form (Appendix E).

Appendix

8. Individual Reminder Cards for basic chores will eventually be replaced by one Morning, one Day, and one Evening Reminder Card.

9. Encourage your child to move the Reminder Cards as soon as a job is completed. The act of hanging the Reminder Card on the Finish Peg creates a sense of accomplishment. This practice will also eliminate a lengthy tally at the end of the day. Bedtime is not the time to determine what chores have been completed.

    A. Do not reward your child for partial jobs.

    B. Do not expect perfection in the beginning. Encourage your child to perform quality work by gradually shaping the behavior you desire.

    C. Assist your child during a particular task, but do not redo a chore. Give your child an approval or ask her to do the chore again.

Melissa was having difficulty getting her four-year old daughter, Sarah, to do her Morning Chores. They established a rule that she could not leave the home or play until her Morning Chores were completed. Often Sarah would not earn a Ticket for completing Morning Chores because she did not get them finished <u>before</u> she left home in the morning.

One morning a play date at the park was set up for Sarah. She was told that if her chores were not done, she would not go. When her friend arrived, Sarah opened the door in her pajamas. Her mother asked if

her Morning Chores were done and Sarah said, "No, but I'll hurry and get them done."

Sara was told they couldn't wait and her face dropped. At first she didn't believe she would not be able to go, but as her friend drove away, she began to cry.

Sarah experienced a difficult lesson as she faced the consequence of her actions, but her mother allowed her to fail so she could learn accountability. Sarah has now become much better about completing chores on time without a reminder.

10. Every morning the *AK* Board is reset. All of the completed chores are returned to the Start Peg. It is the responsibility of your child to reset the board each.

> **HELPFUL HINT:** It is helpful to turn the Reminder Cards over when they are placed on the Finish Peg. This keeps the cards in order and saves time when restarting the board the next day.

Tips for Using Reminder Cards

➤ Your child's chores should be age appropriate.
➤ Core Chores can be added, combined, or deleted throughout the program.
➤ If your child is having difficulty completing Core Chores, reassess the program and add or delete chores as needed.

➢ Your child should not be forced to complete chores. It is important to simply provide choices and consequences.

➢ The blank cards can help you create unique reminders for your child.

Earning Tickets

Your child earns Tickets by completing basic or Core Chores. Tickets can then be used to buy privileges and activities. Children learn that privileges are earned, not given. The *AK* program becomes effective as your child attaches value to Tickets.

It is important to take sufficient time in the beginning to teach your child the specific requirements for earning, using, and losing Tickets to avoid confusion and hurt feelings. It is also essential to let your child know what specific activities have now become Ticketed Activities and will require a Ticket before they can be enjoyed. Help your child learn what activities require a Ticket by posting a list or pictures of all Ticketed Activities (See Appendix E).

Appendix

HELPFUL HINT: Keep unearned Tickets accessible by hanging them on a hook above the *AK* Board or on the refrigerator.

to Earning Tickets

1. Your child earns one Ticket for every color grouping of chores completed.

    A. One Ticket is earned if *all* Morning Chores (yellow bars) are completed, one Ticket if *all* Day chores (red bars) are completed, and one Ticket if *all* Evening Chores (blue bars) are completed. Three Tickets can be earned each day for completing all Core Chores.

    B. All the chores in one color grouping must be completed to receive a Ticket for that color. For example, if your child completes all of his Morning Chores, except one, acknowledge the chores that were completed, but a Ticket is not earned. Nothing is taken away, but nothing is given.

    C. As soon as the color grouping of chores is completed, your child receives one Ticket. This provides immediate reinforcement for positive behavior.

    D. Earned Tickets are placed on the Ticket Peg.

    E. Tickets can be used only after they are earned.

HELPFUL HINT: A child may not value Tickets until they are linked to something desirable. As Tickets are paired with a privilege, they become a primary reinforcement and become valuable.

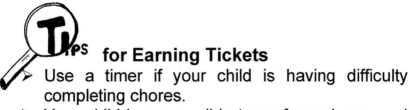

for Earning Tickets

➤ Use a timer if your child is having difficulty completing chores.

➤ Your child is responsible to perform chores and let you know when they are completed.

➤ Encourage your child to use Tickets when they are earned.

Using Tickets

Using Tickets to buy activities and privileges empowers your child to make decisions, engage in positive behaviors, and limit idle activities. The *Accountable Kids* program extinguishes *entitlement* because privileges are earned instead of expected or demanded. Children begin to see that effort earns valued activities and empowers them to make decisions. Nothing extra is provided in the *AK* program. The privileges children earn are the same ones that were previously given.

Suggestions for Ticketed Activities

1. Television
2. Movies
3. Video games
4. Videos
5. Computer
6. Art projects
7. Playing with friends
8. Sleepovers
9. Playing at the park
10. Swimming
11. Riding a bike
12. Flying kites
13. Trampoline time
14. Board games
15. Outings to the library
16. Phone calls
17. Extra book reading
18. Later bedtime
19. Back rub
20. Listening to music
21. Going on a field trip

 **for Using Tickets**

1. Many of the activities your child enjoys become Ticketed Activities in the *AK* program. This means a Ticket is required every time your child wants to participate in the activity.

    A. It is important that Ticketed Activities require a Ticket every time or not at all. *Consistency* is vital to the *AK* program.

    B. A Ticketed Activity must be something your child wants to do, instead of something you want him to do. Your child must be willing to pay for the activity.

    C. A Ticket can be charged for spontaneous activities. If a friend calls and wants your child to go ice-skating, a Ticket could be required.

2. Your child is responsible to provide Tickets for *all* Ticketed Activities. If a Ticket is not given before enjoying the activity, an additional Ticket is also charged. Progress will be sabotaged if your child is allowed to have any of the predetermined Ticketed Activities before earning and paying for the privilege. If watching a movie requires a Ticket, then charge a Ticket *every time* for this activity.

"I am no longer a television police officer. The Accountable Kids program has helped my children limit television on their own. They know that one-half hour of television costs one Ticket. If they go over that time, they owe me one more Ticket. The great part is, I make them accountable for how much time has passed. My son actually uses a timer so it won't cost him another Ticket. My children work hard for their Tickets, and they use them sparingly. They have become more selective in their television choices since they have had to monitor their viewing by paying Tickets." S.E.

HELPFUL HINT: Avoid using food as a Ticketed Activity. This might transcend into more serious problems.

3. If your child runs out of Tickets, it is important for your child to earn more before a Ticketed Activity can be enjoyed. This will eliminate pleading and encourage planning. It may be necessary for your child to miss out on something important, but only in this way can consistency be maintained and a valuable lesson learned.

"My oldest boy is very good about paying for privileges before enjoying them. He asks for Tickets when they are earned and gives them without a reminder. My daughter struggles with this concept. She is continually forgetting to pay for privileges.

To help her understand the importance of paying before using, we established a rule that two Tickets are charged for any Ticketed Activity which is not paid for ahead of time. One Ticket is taken for the activity and one Ticket for not paying before beginning. Now my daughter remembers to pay for privileges because she experiences a consequence if she does not." J.S.

4. You have the final vote on when and how your child's Tickets are used. If your child wants to buy something inappropriate, you have the right to veto the idea. You do not have to explain yourself or argue the point. If your answer is no, make it so.

5. One optional part of this program is to select one day of the week as a *'Free Day'*. On this day your child's activities and privileges are not limited. Creating a Free Day prepares your child to graduate to the next step of accountability where Tickets and Reminder Cards are replaced by internal discipline and written agreements.

   A. On Free Days Tickets are not earned, used, or lost.

   B. Chores are still required to be completed.

   C. Free Days create a testing time to observe how your child applies the principles of the program without using the external components. Discuss balance and self discipline on this day.

"Our son has AD/HD and is benefiting from the structure and consistency of the Accountable Kids program. We decided to make one day our 'free day' to see how our family would do without being limited with chore boards and Tickets. On Saturdays our children are allowed to freely enjoy television, video games, and other Ticketed Activities as long as their chores are done.

My son is especially susceptible to headaches. He tends to get more headaches on Saturdays because he over stimulates himself with television and video games. This has been a great learning time for my son and the entire family. We are personally experiencing the effects of over using privileges.

Each Saturday gets a little better, but we are all glad to start the Accountable Kids program on Sunday. My children are enjoying the benefits of using a program that helps us work together as a family and grow as individuals." K.L.

Tips for Using Tickets

➢ Ticketed Activities require a Ticket every time.
➢ Privileges are earned, not given.
➢ Whenever possible, your child has control over how Tickets will be used.
➢ It is most effective if your child does not begin the day with more than two Tickets.
➢ Encourage your child to use Tickets throughout the day.

Best Behavior Card

George Washington gave advice over two hundred years ago that still holds true today. He stated, "Virtue is harder to be got than knowledge; and if lost in a young man, it is seldom recovered." He further stated, "All education is the education of character" (Bennett, 1998). The purpose of the *AK* program is not only to teach children accountability and responsibility, but to train their hearts and minds to embrace integrity, honesty, compassion, respect, and perseverance.

The Best Behavior Card encourages values and virtues on a daily basis. The Best Behavior Card acknowledges positive behaviors such as being kind and helpful, performing acts of service, being honest, expressing love, and displaying caring acts. Receiving the Best Behavior Card builds self-confidence and self-esteem in children.

Best Behavior Cards are given to encourage positive character traits, helping children believe in themselves,

increasing their self worth, and experiencing that they are capable and competent. Best Behavior Cards help older children internalize values and develop a sense of identity and purpose.

Throughout the program you will be presented with opportunities to assist your child in developing positive character traits. Celebrate these times! It takes time and dedication to instill values and morals. The Best Behavior Card helps you focus on your child's successes and positive strides. Each time you give your child a Best Behavior Card it opens the door for communication and thought provoking comments that can lead to enhanced relationships, moral development, and internal reflection.

One of the key components in successful parenting is the quality of the bond between parent and child. The *AK* program supplies tools to help build successful relationships through modeling and encouraging positive behaviors and values.

Encouragement vs. Praise

Best Behavior Cards help parents encourage their child's positive behavior. Encouragement is given to make a child feel valued, worthy, and capable of improvement. It may seem subtle, but there is a large difference between praise and encouragement. When a parent *praises*, his words directly link the behavior to the child. For example, a parent that praises a child for cleaning his room might say, "Thank you for cleaning your room; you are such a good boy. I love you." These words imply that the boy is loved and is good because he cleaned his room. The child may conclude that to get love and to be good, he must have a clean room. If he is ever bad or if his room is not clean, he may wonder if he is still loved.

To *encourage*, use words that acknowledge a child's behavior without connecting it to him. When your child cleans his room say, "Good job!" or "Looks good" or "Way to go." Using these words will let your child know his behavior is good, but the behavior is not required for you to love him.

Words of Encouragement for Accountable Kids

Great Job ♥ Excellent ♥ Terrific ♥ How Thoughtful ♥ That's incredible ♥ Astonishing♥ Take a Bow ♥ Fabulous ♥ Marvelous ♥ Awesome ♥ Tremendous ♥ Inspiring ♥ Breathtaking ♥ Extraordinary Effort ♥ Far Out ♥ Amazing Work ♥ Looks Good♥ Well Done ♥ Way to go ♥ Wonderful ♥ Marvelous ♥ Incredible ♥ Out of this World ♥ Extra Special ♥ Phenomenal ♥ Cool ♥ Bravo ♥ A+ Endeavor ♥ Sensational ♥ Right On ♥ Top Job ♥ #1 Job♥ Nice Going ♥ First Rate Work ♥ Superb ♥ Thumbs Up ♥ Astounding ♥ Brilliant ♥

Encouragement is a wonderful way to help your child feel valued and loved, but it can also prove detrimental if overused or used in an inappropriate manner. A child that receives constant and continual encouragement can become addicted to this type of reinforcement and never develops his own internal motivation and direction. It is important for parents to encourage children, but encouragement should not be the driving force to promote positive behavior.

A mother was talking about the power of positive praise. She believed the success of her family stemmed from continuous, constant praise and encouragement. She said that over the years she never had to take a child out of her church service for discipline problems. She spent the entire service complimenting her children on how well they were doing. She kept busy directing them in positive ways.

This type of parenting can create an atmosphere where children become addicted to praise. As the children develop, constant praise may prove detrimental to their individual growth.

As her children enter the work force, their supervisors will probably not be willing to continue the same type of motivation and praise necessary to keep them directed and focused. In real life, friends, spouses, and co-workers usually will not put a great deal of time and attention into praise. If this is what a person needs to succeed, he is set up for failure in the real world.

 **to Using Best Behavior Cards**

1. The Accountable Kids program includes Best Behavior Cards to encourage values, virtues, morals, and life skills.

    A. Hang the Best Behavior Cards with your child's unearned Tickets.

    B. A Best Behavior Card can be given for a specific value the family is working on, or it can be given for a spontaneous act that deserves recognition.

    C. A Best Behavior Card is not earned if requested.

2. Best Behavior cards are earned when a child displays positive values or virtues. A Best Behavior form is provided to specify the behaviors and values you wish to encourage (Appendix E).

Appendix

3. Best Behavior Cards are used as Tickets.

> **HELPFUL HINT:** This is not an *all or nothing* program. If you take a break from the program, it is easy to begin fresh the next day.

Suggested Values and Virtues

1.	Integrity	13.	Trust
2.	Honesty	14.	Gratitude
3.	Charity	15.	Responsibility
4.	Morality	16.	Friendship
5.	Respect	17.	Faith
6.	Love	18.	Work ethics
7.	Self-discipline	19.	Perseverance
8.	Cooperation	20.	Reverence
9.	Compassion	21.	Loyalty
10.	Kindness	22.	Humility
11.	Good manners	23.	Empathy
12.	Courage		

AIM FOR THE STARS

The Best Behavior Card is a specific tool that parents can use to encourage children in a balanced and healthy manner, however there are numerous other ways for children to receive encouragement in the *AK* program. Children receive internal satisfaction by placing the Reminder Cards on the Finish Peg, earning and using Tickets, completing chores, going on Special Dates, and earning Bonus Bucks.

for Using Best Behavior Cards

➤ Do not overuse the Best Behavior Card, but use it with awareness to recognize praiseworthy virtues periodically.

➤ The Best Behavior Card is an intermittent reinforcement designed to sustain positive behaviors.

➤ You can create a special weekly drawing with earned Best Behavior Cards. The winner can select something out of a grab bag or receive a pre-selected incentive.

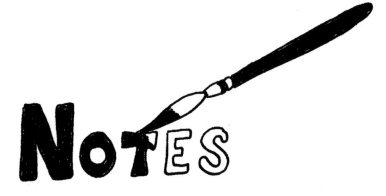

Disciplining with Tickets

The *Accountable Kids* discipline program provides an avenue to impose negative consequences firmly and compassionately without physical contact or losing control. Parents using the *AK* program model appropriate ways to express emotions. This helps children develop the emotional awareness necessary to develop self-control, empathy, and respect for others. Children experience real world consequences in a safe environment.

It is important for parents to let their children know they are happy, sad, frustrated, angry, or embarrassed so their children begin to understand that their behavior impacts others. If parents exhibit appropriate avenues to deal with difficult emotions, children can learn appropriate ways to express emotions by watching and then imitating their parents.

Taking Tickets for negative behaviors allows parents to discipline a child in a manner that is respectful, yet effective. Taking Tickets away in a consistent and firm manner can eliminate negative behaviors. It is effective when a child learns that negative behaviors result in negative consequences and positive behaviors result in positive consequences. This shifts the responsibility from the parent to the child. A major goal of this program is to change a child's idea of discipline into self-discipline.

Suggestions for Negative Behaviors Resulting in the loss of a Ticket

1. Lying
2. Hitting
3. Arguing
4. Fighting
5. Tantrums
6. Disrespect
7. Using bad language
8. Rude gestures or actions
9. Problems at School
10. Being told twice to do something
11. Asking for something after being told no
12. Not completing a Core Chore
13. Not completing homework
14. Asking one parent for something that has been declined by the other

Sandy constantly pouted when she was upset. She would put her nose in the air, throw her hands down, scrunch her face, and sigh with contempt as she stomped away. When her family started using the AK program, Sandy was told that whenever she displayed this unpleasant behavior she would not be given a warning, but would immediately lose a Ticket.

From then on, every time Sandy pouted her parents calmly asked her for a Ticket. Sandy's parents would ask her why she lost the Ticket, how pouting made her feel, and how she thought her parents felt when she made an unpleasant face. Her parents were consistent, and after the first week the negative behavior declined dramatically. A short time later, the negative behavior was completely eliminated. Sandy learned that her behavior did not serve her, and in fact harmed her.

HELPFUL HINT: Let the first day be a trial run. Point out instances when your child would lose a Ticket, but don't actually take one until day two.

 **to Disciplining with Tickets**

1. Understand the behavioral stage of your child before establishing rules and consequences.

Matt is in the preoperational stage. He had been told by his father not to go inside the house with muddy feet while lunch was being prepared. When Matt stepped inside the door, his father reprimanded him and sent him back outside. Matt was hungry, and a few minutes later walked in the house to see if lunch was ready. His father looked up in exasperation and said, "What part of 'No' do you not understand?" Matt looked at his father in a puzzled, hurt manner.

This type of reprimand is confusing to a preoperational child. It requires the child to reverse the logic because the question is not direct. Preoperational children benefit from short, direct questions and discussions. Questioning a preoperational child in an indirect manner can be frustrating for the parent as well as the child.

When the father remembered the developmental stage of his child, he began asking direct questions and kept all reprimands short and simple. He stopped giving multiple warnings, and Matt learned to respond the first time or experience a consequence.

HELPFUL HINT: Keep it simple! Keep it short! When a young child gets in trouble, tell him what he did wrong, invoke a consequence, and move on. Only discuss situations in depth as your child progresses to the operational and formal operational stages.

---

2. Explain to your child that Tickets are lost for undesirable behavior.

 A. There are <u>NO</u> second or third chances. Once your child has been warned the behavior is unacceptable, a Ticket is lost if the behavior is repeated.

 B. If many warnings are given, your child will learn that the offense can be repeated without a consequence. This type of inconsistent discipline will actually encourage negative behavior.

A family was experiencing problems with their children watching television and playing video games when chores and homework weren't completed. Each time the children were caught watching television, they would receive a stern lecture and the television would be turned off as punishment.

The parents began using the AK program and discovered that simply turning the television off was not a punishment. Their children only lost a privilege they should not have had. The parents established a rule that privileges could only be bought if all chores and homework were completed. If a child enjoyed a Ticketed Activity before paying for the privilege two Tickets would be charged. One Ticket was charged for the privilege, one Ticket was lost for not pr-paying. The children's behavior quickly changed because they experienced a consequence.

3. Discuss behaviors that will cause your child to lose a Ticket. Establish clear consequences for negative behaviors and post a reference using the *Tickets Lost* form (Appendix E).

Appendix

4. When your child loses a Ticket, act respectfully. If you remain neutral about the consequence, the child will be more likely to focus on the problem instead of blaming you. If your child attempts to avoid responsibility, simply restate the rules that have been established.

"I have an eleven year old daughter who is very grumpy in the mornings. She was often sent away from the breakfast table for being rude and negative. She would commonly go to her room and continue to escalate the behavior until I got involved. I would let her know that if she didn't stop her behavior there would be another consequence. In my mind, I was wondering what my next step would be.

We have been using the Accountable Kids program for over six months. I no longer send my daughter to her room for poor behavior, I just ask for a Ticket. If she protests, she loses another Ticket. She has lost up to four Tickets for one outbreak. Once she learned her behavior cost her Tickets, her attitude became much better. I didn't realize that I was actually rewarding her negative behavior with my attention.

Now, I don't get emotional when I take a Ticket. My daughter has learned her choices bring positive and negative consequences. I have been liberated from being the mean mom." M.N.

HELPFUL HINT: If your child is repeating a negative behavior, a pay off is being received.

5. If your child displays a negative behavior and does not have a Ticket to take away, decide on an alternate disciplinary measure. Make certain your child knows what this measure is beforehand. For example, you may decide to use a timeout or the loss of a privilege when your child does not have a Ticket left to take.

TESTING LIMITS

   A. After your child has tested the limits of the *AK* program, you will rarely have to use an alternative form of discipline.

   B. The primary consequence of not having Tickets is the loss of all privileges or Ticketed Activities until your child earns more Tickets. This restriction of privileges can be an effective means of discipline and can motivate your child to work, earn, and behave in the future.

C. Some children test the program. It is not uncommon for negative behaviors to get worse before they get better. Failure is an important component in learning. Continue to be consistent. Provide positive consequences for positive behaviors and negative consequences for negative behaviors.

HELPFUL HINT: Allow your child to encounter the consequence of not having Tickets to experience learning and growth.

6. Do not threaten or give second chances. Don't talk about discipline measures. If you say it, do it.
   A. Teach your child you will do what you say.
   B. Make certain your consequence is something that you can, and are willing to, enforce.

> *"One day my nephew got in trouble for throwing food in the car. His mother gave him a warning and threatened a five-minute timeout if he repeated the offense. My nephew continued to throw French fries at his sister, and his upcoming punishment grew. Finally in a moment of frustration, his mom threatened that he would be grounded 'forever' if he threw one more piece of food. My nephew tested the limits by throwing his last French fry. His mom angrily reaffirmed his lifetime sentence of being grounded.*
>
> *Unfortunately, he never spent one minute in timeout. He knew his mom would not follow through with her outrageous threat. He was learning at a very young age to not trust what his mother said.*

It made me wonder if he would doubt her words at other times. When she told him she loved him or he did a great job, would he trust her to tell the truth?" C.N.

Tips to Disciplining with Tickets

➢ Be consistent!
➢ Discipline with respect.
➢ Do not discount another parent or responsible adult in front of your child.

HELPFUL HINT: The details of the program may seem overwhelming if you read the entire Four Step program at one time. Remember, each step is only introduced to your child after the previous concepts are learned.

Teaching Moments

Teaching moments occur when your child loses a Ticket. Children experience that negative behavior results in negative consequences. They learn to label the specifics of how others feel about their behavior. This is the basis for true empathy. If guided correctly, children also begin to understand their own emotions and build a repertoire of healthy responses to use during conflict.

1. If a problem occurs, take time to ask simple, direct questions after your child is calm. For example, if your son hits his sister you could ask, "How did you feel when you hit your sister? How do you think mommy felt when you hit your sister? Can you think of a different way to handle the situation?" Your child's answers can begin to guide him toward understanding the perspective of others.

2. Let your child know how you feel when you take a Ticket for negative behaviors. Avoid directing frustration directly towards your child. This helps your child become aware of specific emotions and deal with them in an appropriate manner.

3. When your child hands over the Ticket ask why the Ticket was lost. This reminds your child that the negative choice resulted in a negative consequence.

4. Resolve all parental disagreements away from your child. If there is a family problem, deal with it as a family.

5. Create a united front in parenting. Avoid letting your child divert attention away from problem ownership.

"Our son, Jack is very good at directing attention away from himself in times of trouble. Last week Jack got into trouble at school. During a discussion of the problem, my husband began arguing and our son became disinterested and uninvolved in the conversation. Our son had divided us and shifted the attention from him. After using the Accountable Kids program we discuss problems before including our son. We create a united front and then tackle problems

together. Jack is learning to deal with his problems and not divide us as a team." M.T.

6. Discuss the *AK* program with individuals who will be interacting with or caring for your child. It is important that boundaries are consistent to avoid manipulation. The *Fast Track to Accountable Kids* in Appendix F provides a quick reference.

 End of Step

Congratulations!! You've completed Step One of the *AK* program; you are one step closer to raising an Accountable Kid. Proceed to Step Two after your child understands the basic concepts of this step.

HELPFUL HINT: Don't linger in Step One for too long because the next step is exciting and motivating for your child.

Special Date Card & Privilege Pass

Welcome to Step Two of the *Accountable Kids* program. General reminders for Core Chores may still be needed at this time, but you should no longer be directing every task your child completes. He should be experiencing and learning that basic chores are required in order to enjoy basic privileges. At this point your child is ready to take the next step.

Hold a short family meeting to discuss accomplishments and progress. Present Step Two of the *AK* program. A formal family meeting will be discussed in further detail in Chapter Eight.

Special Date Card

The concept of working for *future* rewards is presented with the Special Date Card. Children earn a sticker for the Special Date Card each day all the Core Chores are completed. A Special Date with one parent is enjoyed when the card is filled with ten stickers.

I Earned a
Special Date
With_____

The Special Date Card reinforces the importance of completing Core Chores by providing a specific incentive when *ALL* of the Core Chores are finished. This part of the *Accountable Kids* program has become a favorite component for many parents and children. By consistently implementing this portion of the program, children learn the importance of completing all of their chores and discover they are capable of setting goals and earning rewards in the future.

By consistently spending focused time with a child, a foundation is established for future communication. Special Dates provide an opportunity to discuss sensitive concerns and issues in a safe environment. Children can bring parents into their world by exploring fun and healthy activities together.

Abbey had earned a Special Date, and she chose to go bowling with her dad. The night of their date he came home tired and wanted to relax. It was difficult for him to get excited about going out, but his attitude changed when he saw his daughter dressed and beaming with anticipation.

Afterward, he commented that he was surprised how much their date meant to both of them. Although they often spent time together, something was different when they were on their Special Date alone. During their date, Abbey shared many thoughts. They both came home with a feeling of love and closeness. Abbey's dad was convinced that their future dates would keep the communication lines open.

to using the Special Date Card

1. Discuss the requirements for earning a sticker for the Special Date Card.

    A. All Core Chores for the *entire day* must be completed to earn a sticker.

    B. When each box on the card is filled (10 stickers), a Special Date with a parent is earned.

HELPFUL HINT: You may decide to require only five stickers for the first Special Date. Your child may struggle to complete all the Core Chores in the beginning and achieving the Special Date may appear unattainable.

2. Discuss various activities that can be earned by completing the Special Date Card. The possibilities are limitless and often free. This is a time to be creative. Often, the activity is secondary to time spent together in a focused manner. If the activity costs money, remind your child the activity must fit within the family budget.

3. Parents are encouraged to take turns accompanying their child on the Special Date. You may consider occasionally including grandparents.

  A. The Special Date is just for the child that earned the incentive. This is a time for the child and parent to spend one-on-one time together.

  B. Turn off your cell phone and use this time to communicate. Help your child feel important and special by listening and interacting with him.

  C. Allow your child to plan the date. Spend time doing what he considers important and fun.

After Brian completed his Special Date Card, he chose to go hiking with his mom. She was looking forward to spending time alone with Brian, but she wondered if he would really appreciate the date, since they already spent a lot of time together.

She was very surprised at how different Brian was when they were on their special outing. She was able to be attentive, listen, and direct all of her attention to Brian. She learned new things about him, and he shared personal information that brought them closer.

Brian appreciated that his mom would take time to do something that he enjoyed. This opportunity allowed him to develop comfort in being alone with his mom and allowed him to share his thoughts and emotions with her. His mom was pleasantly surprised at how positive Brian was on their date. Their date enabled them to have fun together and take time out for each other.

4. When the Special Date Card is completed, set a date for the activity and go as soon as possible. You can keep track of special outings by using the *Special Date Log* (See Appendix E).

5. Begin a new Special Date Card.

Appendix

HELPFUL HINT: Avoid taking anyone else on the Special Date with you. This is a time to build and enhance your relationship with your child. The dynamics of the date will change with another individual.

Tips for the Special Date Card

➢ Set a goal to have at least one date per month with your child.
➢ Date cards can be re-used.
➢ Your child decides what to do on her special date, if possible. You can give suggestions, but remember this is her reward.
➢ Your child only earns a sticker if all the Core Chores are completed for that day.
➢ Hang the stickers on or near the AK Board.

Suggestions for Special Dates

- ♥ Stargazing
- ♥ Dinner and a movie
- ♥ Play miniature golf
- ♥ Hit golf balls at the driving range
- ♥ Bike riding
- ♥ Go bowling
- ♥ Engage in a game of paintball
- ♥ Play laser tag
- ♥ Ride go-carts
- ♥ Play tennis
- ♥ Go to a sporting event
- ♥ Attend a concert
- ♥ Make a creative craft project
- ♥ Start a small garden with your child
- ♥ Visit an amusement park
- ♥ Spend the evening at the arcade
- ♥ Go for ice cream
- ♥ Take a scenic drive
- ♥ Visit a museum
- ♥ Enjoy an adventure walk at the zoo
- ♥ Take a nature walk
- ♥ Have an old fashioned cook out

- ♥ Enjoy a night at the circus
- ♥ Plan a day of cross country skiing
- ♥ Go fishing
- ♥ Have dinner at a drive-in restaurant
- ♥ Go hiking
- ♥ Head for the dirt in an off road vehicle
- ♥ Ride horses
- ♥ Rent a seat on a horse and buggy ride
- ♥ Book a hot air balloon ride
- ♥ Go ice skating
- ♥ Go roller blading in the park
- ♥ Visit the planetarium
- ♥ Be brave and learn to rappel
- ♥ Enjoy a rodeo
- ♥ Find new terrain on a snowmobile
- ♥ Learn a new style of dancing
- ♥ Have a pizza party
- ♥ Enjoy adventures in bird watching
- ♥ Go see a ballet

- ♥ Enjoy a musical
- ♥ Go to a dinner theater
- ♥ Splash around at the water park
- ♥ Compete in a game of pool
- ♥ Make up a treasure hunt
- ♥ Enjoy a hayride
- ♥ Sip hot cocoa while ice fishing
- ♥ Go sailing
- ♥ Plan a beach party
- ♥ Take a pottery class
- ♥ Play at the park

- ♥ Bathe in a hot spring
- ♥ Hit the batting cages
- ♥ Put on warm clothes and go sledding
- ♥ Work on a scrapbook
- ♥ Record a book on tape together
- ♥ Make a video to show to the family
- ♥ Play board games
- ♥ Cook a special meal

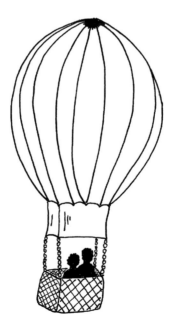

The Privilege Pass

The Privilege Pass is an incentive designed to eliminate a specific negative behavior. It is designed to empower children to predict consequences, follow rules, and redirect themselves toward positive behaviors. Your child earns the Privilege Pass when he displays a predetermined positive behavior. The Privilege Pass can be used for specific privileges or activities. It can motivate your child to go to bed without problems, complete homework on time, improve poor behavior at the dinner table, keep a room clean, get up without reminders, and improve manners and language.

Jake is an only child and his parents are very involved in his life. They were not certain if all of the aspects of the AK program would be beneficial, but they committed to follow all four steps and use the suggested tools.

Jake's parents were pleasantly surprised to see how well the program worked in their home. They saw long term benefits to every component in the program. They especially liked the Privilege Pass because it provided quick results and encouraged Jake to improve his table manners. Each night at dinner he had the ability to earn a Privilege Pass which granted him a special game with his dad. The Privilege Pass helped eliminate a specific negative behavior in a positive and fun way for Jake.

This is a fun part of the program! The Privilege Pass can buy privileges and activities just like a Ticket, but it can also purchase special privileges that regular Tickets cannot buy. The Privilege Pass earns something special that can be given on a daily basis. The incentive should be something that motivates your child to change the behavior. The incentive can be changed at any time so your child continues to be motivated.

HELPFUL HINT: The key to the Privilege Pass is motivation. Make certain the incentive is something for which your child is willing to work.

 to Using the Privilege Pass

1. Determine the behavior you want to change. It could be going to bed easily, completing homework, displaying good table manners, getting up in the morning without problems, etc. Be specific about the positive behavior that will *replace* the undesirable behavior.

2. Explain to your child that the Privilege Pass is used to buy a special privilege. Discuss the different activities that only the Privilege Pass will afford.

3. List the exact requirements for earning and using the Privilege Pass. A form is provided to act as a reference (See Appendix E).

Appendix

95

4. When your child successfully achieves the desired behavior, a Privilege Pass is earned. Incentives are most effective if they are received immediately. If the Pass is earned for a bedtime behavior, place it on the Progress Board so it will be seen in the morning.

Bailey had been looking forward to spending a few days with her cousins out of town. During the day she was happy, but each night she would become very homesick. Her Aunt Judy tried to console her, but each night Bailey's crying would escalate to uncontrollable sobbing. Aunt Judy finally called Bailey's mom for suggestions.

Bailey's family had been using the Accountable Kids program in their home for six months. Her mom wondered if the AK concepts that worked at home would be helpful. She suggested letting Bailey earn a Privilege Pass if she went to bed without crying or getting up.

Bailey's bedtime experience dramatically changed. Aunt Judy called the next morning and said Bailey went to bed calmly and happily. Aunt Judy couldn't believe the power of the Privilege Pass.

Bailey told her mom she wanted to use her Privilege Pass to paint when they returned home. Because her parents knew the importance of reinforcing Bailey's positive behavior as soon as possible, they put dinner plans on hold and spent time together painting as soon as they got home.

Bailey had learned to display positive behaviors and delay her immediate wants for delayed rewards. The AK program empowered Bailey to make good choices and experience positive consequences.

5. The Privilege Pass will not always be tied to the same behavior problem. The goal is to help your child develop positive habits. After the appropriate positive behavior becomes ingrained, the learned behavior can be sustained by changing the continuous and immediate incentive (Privilege Pass) to an intermittent reinforcement (Best Behavior Card). The Best Behavior Card can then reinforce and sustain the new learned behavior, while the Privilege Pass is used to work on another problem behavior.

Beth was having trouble getting her two children to bed on time without problems. She had tried a variety of tactics with limited success. Beth decided to put the Privilege Pass to the test. Her children loved to read books at night and enjoyed the stories she had recorded on tape. Beth explained that they would have the opportunity to earn a Privilege Pass every night by staying in bed and remaining quiet. This meant they would need to take care of all of their needs before climbing in bed. Beth told them that by going to bed in this way, they would earn a Privilege Pass that would be good for reading extra books, listening to books on tape or nighttime stories the next night.

The Privilege Pass provided the incentive for Beth's children to change their behavior. They learned to go to bed in a positive manner habitually. She then started using the Privilege Pass to encourage good table manners. Beth now gives her children a Best Behavior Card periodically to sustain and reinforce going to bed without problems.

Tips for the Privilege Pass

➤ The Privilege Pass can be used only *after* it is earned.

➤ There are <u>no</u> exceptions or second chances. If any excuses are allowed for not following the rules, a system of arguing, explaining, justification, and judging will be created. This is sometimes difficult when your child produces a reasonable excuse, but remember your child is not being punished for negative behavior; he is being rewarded for positive behavior.

➤ The incentive for the Privilege Pass can be changed periodically to match your child's interests.

"*My children are excited to start the Privilege Pass this week. We decided that if they woke up on their own, with a pleasant attitude, they would earn a Privilege Pass. Jesse decided the Privilege Pass would be good for playing the piano with me and Nick selected a hand-foot massage or listening to music. These are all things they love to do. My children are now empowered to focus on positive behaviors and motivated to change negative behaviors.*"

They are really looking forward to this. I have mixed emotions because it will require more planning on my part, but I know how much it will mean to them . . . I'm willing. I'm happy though, because it will encourage me to do what I've really wanted to do, and yet just haven't taken the time." J.W.

 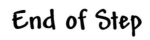 

End of Step

Congratulations!! You have completed Step Two of the *Accountable Kids* program. You are one step closer to raising an Accountable Kid. When your child understands the concepts of this step, proceed to Step Three of the program.

Extra Chores & Savings

Welcome to Step Three of the *Accountable Kids* program. In this step, children experience the benefits of completing extra jobs and the rewards of serving others. They learn to manage money by earning Bonus Bucks for completing Extra Chores. Bonus Bucks empower children to purchase the items they desire.

The AK program motivates children to complete Extra Chores and to appreciate the value of money. Instead of following the traditional allowance system, the *AK* program provides an avenue to reward children based on effort rather than existence. This process empowers children to make decisions regarding the earning, spending, and saving of money. Extra Chores

101

are now added to enable children to earn money to buy or save for the things they desire. At this time, a specific Reminder Card is introduced to encourage helping others each day. The Helping Hands card reinforces the basic idea of serving others without monetary rewards. Parents can use this card to balance the two concepts of working for money and working for service. Children learn that helping others can be rewarding in itself.

Extra Chores

The *AK* program teaches children that every member of the home has responsibilities as well as privileges. In this program there are basic chores children are responsible to complete each day in order to enjoy the benefits of living in the home. It is important for children to know that everyone in the family does chores. It may be helpful to point out the various chores that the contributing members of the family do every day.

> "My son asked me when he would be old enough to stop doing chores. He believed that I didn't have chores. I pointed out that I had many chores to complete. I explained that cooking, washing dishes, grocery shopping, and taking care of the house were my chores. I showed him my checklist that reminded me what I needed to do. I told him he could help me with my chores instead of doing his own if he would prefer. After a short while, he asked if he could have his own chores back." M.S.

The *AK* program teaches that completing Core Chores provides basic privileges within the home, but it does not buy treats, toys, games, or activities that require money. Children can earn money for these extras by completing Extra Chores. Paying children for Extra Chores is not designed to offer excessive amounts of spending money, but rather it is to provide an avenue to pay for more personal expenses. As a child becomes more adept at completing chores, parents can begin to place an emphasis on quality instead of quantity, thus teaching another valuable life lesson.

A child eventually develops the desire to have money and wants the ability to make decisions about purchases. Extra Chores are added to enable children to earn money for the extra things in life. If there is a deficit in a child's life, Extra Chores are a way to fill it. If a child lacks nothing, there is no motivation to complete further responsibilities. Extra Chores provide a feeling of empowerment, self-confidence, and independence.

Chris thrived on a system of structure and incentives. He woke up every morning and hurried through all of his chores. As soon as he got home he would run around and complete as many *Extra Chores* as possible. In the evening his parents finally had to set a time when *Extra Chores* must be completed so he would get ready for bed. He earned a lot of *Bonus Bucks* throughout the week. His parents were a little nervous that his efforts would cost more than they could afford.

As Chris earned more *Bonus Bucks*, his parents held Chris more financially accountable. They began letting him pay for clothes, school pictures, piano lessons, and basic supplies for school and home. Together they opened a savings account where a certain amount of his earnings went toward his college fund. Finally, his parents redefined his *Core Chores* to include more difficult jobs. They also began to emphasize the <u>quality</u> in his work instead of <u>quantity</u>. Chris thrived on this system and gained confidence and self-worth.

 **for Extra Chores**

1. Select appropriate Extra Chores for your child.
   A. Place the Extra Chore cards on the last peg of the Chore Board.
   B. Encourage Extra Chores to be completed any time of the day.

Barbara was at the store with her son Carson. Carson saw a video he really wanted and began asking *her to buy it. Barbara considered the purchase, but knew their finances were limited. Carson pleaded for his mom to change her mind. She told him he could buy the video with his own money if it was important to him. He was told the video cost $19.95.*

His mom smiled inwardly as she watched him weigh the options available to him. Carson had learned the value of earning money in the AK program and was now empowered to make decisions about how he spent it. Carson repeated the price several times before saying, "Mom, it's just not worth that much money." R.S.

2. The last two color bars on the Reminder Cards can distinguish between <u>weekly</u> and <u>daily</u> Extra Chores, <u>paid</u> and <u>non-paid</u> Extra Chores, or <u>rotating</u> and <u>constant</u> Extra Chores. This provides a way to further customize the program to your child as she progresses in the program.

    A.   Extra Chores can be mandatory or optional. They can rotate periodically or remain constant from day to day.

    B.   It is helpful to make assignments on the *My Extra Chores* form to list out your child's weekly and daily chores (Appendix E).

Appendix

HELPFUL HINT: Parents commonly use the purple bar to represent daily Extra Chores and the green bar to represent weekly Extra Chores.

3. Bonus Bucks are given for Extra Chores.

A. Your child receives **Tickets for Core Chores** and **Bonus Bucks for Extra Chores.**

B. Designate the value of your Bonus Bucks. They may be worth whatever you feel is appropriate.

4. After your child completes an Extra Chore, the Reminder Card is hung on the Finish Peg.

A. Your child receives the appropriate amount of Bonus Bucks at the end of the day.

B. Bonus Bucks are given only if all of the Core Chores are completed. This reinforces the importance of completing basic responsibilities.

Kenta went to the store with her four year old daughter, Aly. While standing in the checkout line Aly saw a tube of clear lip-gloss she wanted. Kenta thought it was unimportant and wouldn't buy Aly the lip-gloss. Aly protested and was informed by her mom that the discussion was over.

Aly became very quiet and said, "Mom, will you at least ask the lady how many Bonus Bucks the lip-gloss is?" Kenta was surprised by her daughter's request, but she turned to the cashier and learned the purchase price was $1.99.

Aly got very excited and said, "Oh mom, I have two Bonus Bucks. That's enough to buy the lip-gloss." In that moment Kenta realized that Accountable Kids had given her daughter something very important. Aly was empowered!! She had the ability to make decisions, to *experience the result of hard work, and weigh her options. Aly happily walked out of the store with her new purchase.*

5. If a required Extra Chore is not completed, parents can assign this job to another person. When a job is assigned to the new person he is officially hired with the uncooperative child's money. Families can use the *Hired Help* form to keep track of this work (See Appendix E).

Appendix

6. Provide opportunities for your child to earn additional money by creating a list with specific jobs to help out the family. There is an *Opportunity List* form to list requirements for this work (Appendix E).

> *"Our family went to a large amusement park to celebrate my daughter's sixth birthday. She had been earning extra money for the trip. In the past, we have been bombarded with requests for souvenirs. To our surprise, our daughter carefully looked at the items in the gift stores but never asked for or purchased anything the first day. She knew how much money she had and wanted to see everything before making a decision. She selected her souvenirs carefully, asking how much each item cost. It was refreshing to walk into a store and not continually reject requests.*
>
> *Then she did something unexpected with her last two dollars. She bought her cousin a birthday gift. As she presented the gift to her cousin she said, "Enjoy it, it's all yours."*
>
> *My daughter felt the joy of earning money, the empowerment of providing for her needs, and the enjoyment of sharing what she earned with another. We felt a lump in our throats as we watched her share her*

earnings. We knew she had learned a valuable lesson about giving and receiving." K.S.

Tips for Extra Chores

- ➢ If an Extra Chore is worth more than one Bonus Buck, mark the back of the Chore Card to indicate how much your child will earn by completing the job.
- ➢ Earned Bonus Bucks can be stored on the Savings Peg or put in a separate location until payday.
- ➢ Exchange Bonus Bucks for money once a week.

Helping Hands

The *AK* Reminder Cards are task specific. Parents define the exact requirements for each chore and teach their child what is required for the chore to be considered complete. The Helping Hands Reminder

Card is the only task that is *not* specific to any particular job. This card helps a child become aware of others and encourages him to seek out ways to help around the home. This process helps your child experience the benefits of service.

 **for Helping Hands**

1. Cut the Helping Hands Card so that the blue bar is on bottom. Helping others is now a Core Chore.

2. Introduce the Helping Hands Reminder Card to your child and discuss the requirements.
    A. Your child earns the card each day for helping others.
    B. Specifically acknowledge the positive efforts that earned the Helping Hands card.

"I love the Helping Hands card. In the past, if I asked my children to do a job, they would want to know what they would get in return. We now require that each child perform at least one Helping Hands act during the day. They do not get their star for the Date Card or receive any Bonus Bucks unless this act is completed. It has eliminated the 'carrot syndrome' where they expected something for every action. My children are actually asking me what they can do to help me. Some days the Helping Hands card is earned for small things, other days we do service projects that require more work for neighbors or friends. My children are experiencing the act of service. They now know that if I ask them to help me, it is an act of service and not a paid job." R.E.

TIPS for Helping Hands

➢ Teach your child that if you ask for help it is not an Extra Chore.

➢ The card may represent one effort or many efforts throughout the day.

Savings

The *AK* program provides a valuable learning opportunity to teach the benefits of saving as children learn to earn, budget, and work for future rewards. When children grow older and become independent, a large portion of their money will need to be used for living expenses such as food, taxes, health costs, and transportation. If the habit of saving is not learned early, it may not be incorporated later in life.

Parents can teach the concept of saving to children at an early age by requiring that a portion of all their money earned be deposited into a savings account.

 **Steps** **to Savings**

1. Open a bank account or keep a ledger for the savings portion, depending on your child's age. Parents can use the provided *Passport Savings* form to keep track of savings (See Appendix E).

Appendix

110

2. Discuss the concept of saving for the future with your child. Set savings goals and discuss the purpose of the savings account.

    A. Decide with your child what percentage of his earnings will go to savings.

    B. Allow your child to make decisions regarding his remaining spending money. Sometimes poor decisions will be made, but it is important to allow your child to stumble and experience consequences. If unwise purchases are made, avoid the temptation to rescue or criticize. Learning often occurs during trials and hard times. Although this might be difficult, the lessons learned at a young age will typically be less expensive than later.

Jack and Suzanne began teaching their three boys to save at an early age. As soon as the boys started to earn money, they were taught to put fifty percent into a long-term savings account, ten percent to a church donation, and the remaining forty percent was theirs to spend.

The parents taught their children at a very young age to save money for the future, make charitable donations,

and work to buy the desired extras. As a result, today each boy has a considerable amount in his savings account. The boys learned to use their money wisely and are prepared to handle money as they become adults.

TIPS for saving

> Set savings goals with your child and review monthly progress.

> Avoid using savings for anything other than the designated purpose.

End of Step **3**

Congratulations!! You have learned the components of Step Three of the *AK* program. You are one step closer to raising an Accountable Kid. When your child understands the concepts of this step, proceed to Step Four.

The Family Forum

If you have been using the *Accountable Kids* program consistently, you should be experiencing many positive benefits in your home. Step Four teaches parents to maintain and maximize the program on a weekly and daily basis by establishing a Family Forum and Quiet Time. Quiet Time is discussed in Chapter Nine.

The Family Forum is a key element in maintaining the *AK* program with strength and fortitude. It is a weekly opportunity to celebrate victories, coordinate schedules, set budgets, solve problems, disperse earnings, and unite together as a family. Consistent use of the Family Forum can create structure and harmony within the home and turn problems into learning opportunities. It is a great time to make new commitments and start the week fresh.

Meeting together as a family is vital to the long-term success of the *AK* program. This is a time where children have an opportunity to voice opinions, create rules, and establish definitive consequences. Family

matters can be discussed in an organized and focused manner. Parents can help to prepare children to live independently by teaching and modeling life skills during these meetings. Children learn that resources are limited and their actions affect the time parents have to spend on positive experiences.

A weekly Family Forum opens and establishes positive lines of communication. If a family learns to communicate on a regular basis, it will be easier for this communication to continue during difficult and stressful times.

After the family becomes comfortable with the basic format, the forum can be customized to suit a family's individual needs. It is helpful to hold a Family Forum at least once a week, but parents can call the family together for short meetings anytime. The meeting can be held any day of the week, but it is important to be consistent.

HELPFUL HINT: The Family Forum is important for families of all sizes. Everyone can benefit from organization, planning, and structure.

 **for Family Forum**

1. Select a day your family will meet for one half to one hour each week.
   A. Choose one parent to head the meeting.
   B. Establish rules and guidelines for your meeting.
   C. Post the *Things to Talk About* form for your family to list discussion items for the Family Forum (see Appendix E).

2. Decide how to open your Family Forum. Use your imagination to create interesting and enjoyable meetings.

3. Create a fun ending. There are many ways to end your Family Forum. You may have a game, treat, song, and/or prayer. Games are an excellent activity to include in your closing because they help bring a family together in an atmosphere of enjoyment. Life lesson games that are simple, directed, and fun can help your entire family become more aware of positive behaviors, build self-esteem, and develop character. Compliment games teach your child the value of complimenting others. You can use one of the following examples or be creative and come up with a game of your own.

   ➢ Spin the Bottle – Spin a bottle and the person it points to is the Star. Have the entire family say all the good things they can about the Star. Take turns and be specific in giving compliments. For example, "Lisa is nice," is a good compliment, but "I liked the way Lisa helped me with my homework when I didn't understand it," is better. You can also change the game to have the one who is the Star say something nice about everyone else.

➤ <u>Beanbag Toss</u> - Toss a beanbag between family  members as a game to initiate compliments. The one with the beanbag says a specific positive compliment about another family member and then throws the beanbag to the next person. This continues until each member has received several compliments.

4. Put together a binder to help organize your meetings. Label the following six sections:
    A. Accountable Kids program
    B. Schedules
    C. Family Rules
    D. Problems & Solutions
    E. Finances
    F. Values and Virtues

5. Keep track of family discussions by using a *Family Forum Agenda* form (see Appendix E). This information may be useful for future meetings.

Appendix

> **HELPFUL HINT:** Discuss only the first two sections during your initial Family Forum. Then introduce one additional section per week until you have included all six segments. Don't overwhelm the family with everything at one time.

Accountable Kids Time

During the Family Forum parents can set goals, address problems, acknowledge achievements, and recommit to accountability. The Family Forum also provides a fresh start and an opportunity to monitor progress, encourage positive behaviors, and discuss ways to eliminate negative behaviors.

1. Encourage your child to bring his Bonus Bucks, Special Date Card, personal calendar, and other related items to the Family Forum. Take time to acknowledge achievements and encourage progress. (Refer to *Personal Progress* form Appendix E).

2. Discuss and assign Extra Chores for the upcoming week.

3. The Family Forum becomes your child's payday. Exchange Bonus Bucks for real money weekly.

A. You may wish to allow younger children to keep and use Bonus Bucks until they express a desire to have money.

B. Encourage your child to use a wallet or small purse to hold his money. Help your child learn responsibility by providing opportunities to take care of money.

4. Items for purchase can be introduced at the Family Forum. Place pre-purchased items in a Bonus Basket with a Ticket value attached. The basket is left in full view during the week so your child can see and work toward a specific item. This works particularly well with young children who are visually motivated. Bonus Bucks can then be used to purchase these items during the Family Forum.

The Spencer family decided to fill a Bonus Basket with items their children could purchase. At the end of the Family Forum, they brought out the Bonus Basket. Each item had a specific price. The children could cash in their Bonus Bucks to purchase items.

Grandma had purchased items for her grandchildren, but rather than simply giving presents, she put them in the Bonus Basket. This not only allowed her to give, but also allowed her the joy of seeing her grandchildren earn items they desired. All of the items in the basket were things the parents or grandparents might simply have given their children in the past, but now the children had the opportunity to earn the items.

The children seemed to take better care of the things they earned and bought, and they were excited about the items they were able to buy. They developed self-confidence in the fact that they could purchase items with their earnings.

Schedule

The Family Forum provides a good time to coordinate the family's schedule and decide who is doing what during the next week. At this time family members can discuss responsibilities, jobs, lessons, rides, special functions, and activities.

1. Provide each member of your family with a calendar to keep track of individual schedules. There should also be one main family calendar posted in a common area. You are *not* responsible for events or obligations that were not discussed and scheduled at the Family Forum. Your child is expected to bring up all activities and functions and schedule them with the family.

HELPFUL HINT: Take advantage of the free calendars that many businesses offer.

2. Use the Family Forum to plan your upcoming week and schedule events in the future. This is a great time to reinforce the idea that resources are limited. Your child learns that time and money need to be scheduled and budgeted as a family to create harmony within the home.

Family Rules

Rules are essential in order for any family to operate smoothly. Parents may establish the basic family rules in the beginning, but it works best when children contribute to this process. There may be times when parents establish boundaries and limitations with which children disagree. This is an opportunity to teach children to abide by the parents' decision and trust that the rule is in their best interest. While there are many times when it is beneficial to compromise and negotiate, there are some things that are non-negotiable.

If there is a family rule, there must also be a clear and consistent consequence for breaking the rule. Keep in mind, family rules are established not simply for the benefit of any one person, but for the good of the entire family.

1. Take care to establish age appropriate rules and consequences and then post these rules as a reminder using the *Family Rules* form (Appendix E).

Appendix

2. A family is not a democracy. Likewise, family rules should not be established by majority decision. You can give children a voice and a vote, but you still have the authority to override your children when appropriate. If a solution to a problem is not appropriate, make suggestions that are fair and applicable.

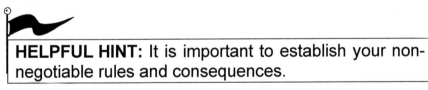

HELPFUL HINT: It is important to establish your non-negotiable rules and consequences.

Problems and Solutions

The success of a family is not measured by whether or not it has problems, but by how those problems are resolved. During the Family Forum family members can address problems, discuss solutions, and suggest rules to establish order in the home. Creating family rules will not eliminate problems, but it will let children know what is expected and exactly what the consequences are. Children still have free agency to abide by the rules or experience the consequences.

HELPFUL HINT: It is helpful if all problems are accompanied by potential solutions.

1. Encourage family members to think through problems before the Family Forum begins.

   A. Teach your child to address the problem and not attack a specific person. All problems should be discussed without using names. For example, Jane may say, "There is a problem with dishes being left on the counter in the kitchen." Jane does not point a finger, which avoids further arguing or justifying. The parent heading the family forum is in charge of keeping all complaints directed and focused.

   B. Ask for suggestions during the Family Forum. Children often have great insight into the problems in the home and can come up with some very good solutions if they are involved.

2. Turn a problem into an opportunity by discussing how your family would operate and feel with the problem eliminated. Help your family visualize the benefits if certain changes were to be implemented.

3. After a problem and solution are presented, the family can put the matter to a vote. If agreed upon, this new solution is added to the family rules and posted.

4. Re-evaluate family rules periodically. Make certain the family rules are achieving the goals of the family.

Finances

During the Family Forum parents can teach children the value of planning, saving, and budgeting. Parents can help their children plan ahead and develop individual budgets. Children can also be involved in assisting with the family budget. In addition to helping children learn financial responsibility,  parents will also reap the rewards of teaching, modeling, and living a life of financial accountability.

It is helpful to divide the finance part of the Family Forum into two sections: Budget and Wish List. Once the family establishes a basic finance plan, this part of the meeting should be quick, easy, and yes . . . fun!

1. Budget –Teach your child to plan ahead by discussing and budgeting finances during the Family Forum.

    A. Help your child establish a personal budget.

    B. Establish a family budget. Take your child's age into account and teach appropriate lessons. This is not the time to burden your child with financial hardships, but it is a good time to teach what is required to run a household.

HELPFUL HINT: Money is only distributed during the Family Forum. Encourage planning and saving by only paying your child once a week.

2. Wish List – Have everyone in the family create a Wish List. The items may be large or small, but they should be something for the *entire family*. Encourage family members to dream about the things they have always wanted the family to purchase.

  A. Select three items your family wants to work toward buying. Encourage family members to shop and find the best price for each item.
  B. Before spending money on a large purchase, discuss the item and compare it against the family Wish List.
  C. Continually update the Wish List. Add new items and take off items purchased or no longer desired. Once a year review the items your family bought through planning and budgeting.

Values and Virtues

The Family Forum provides a great avenue to teach morals, values, and life skills on a weekly basis. The following ideas can be included in the Family Forum to encourage children to embrace positive values and virtues.

1. **Valiant Values** – The *AK* program encourages your child to recognize and develop moral character by selecting a specific value or virtue for your family to focus on for the week. The Valiant Values component of the program is a great reminder for parents to model desired behaviors and lead by example.

A. Select a value or virtue you want your family to focus on each week (refer to page 74 for suggested values and virtues).
B. Encourage family members to notice and compliment others when they observe the selected positive behavior.
C. Award Best Behavior Cards when your child displays a pre-selected value or virtue. Best Behavior Cards can be used as Tickets or placed in a bag for a special weekly drawing.

2. **Secret Service** – Another creative way to help your child develop positive values and virtues is to adopt the Secret Service plan into your family. The Secret Service plan encourages anonymous acts of service between family members.

A. Once a month put the names of family members in a bag. Have everyone draw out one name and keep it a secret.

B. During the month, each family member is encouraged to perform good deeds for the person he is serving without being recognized. It is fun for family members to attempt to figure out who is doing good deeds for them. It is also a challenge to discover new ways to surprise and serve others.

C. At the weekly Family Forum, each family member lists all the Secret Service acts they received during the past week.

D. At the end of the month the identity of each secret family member is revealed and new names are drawn.

> *"The Secret Service plan has been a wonderful addition to our family. My children struggle to get along, and they sometimes focus only on themselves. Secret acts of service help my children remember the needs of other family members. The Secret Service plan also allows my children to experience unconditional acts of love. Each week we remind our children to remember the person they are serving for the month, but we do not force them to do anything specific.*
>
> *Last week my son came to me asking for help. He wanted to make his sister's bed without her knowledge, but he needed help. He was excited to surprise her and enjoyed doing something she would appreciate. When my daughter went into her room, she asked who had made her bed. We said it must have been someone that loved her." C.L.*

Quiet Time

You have learned to organize your family on a weekly and monthly basis during the Family Forum, now it is time to focus on developing methods to bring peace, order, and structure to your family on a daily basis. This is accomplished by observing Quiet Time each day. Quiet Time provides rest and promotes self-control. It is an opportunity to refocus and direct one's self in positive directions. Quiet Time encourages you and your child to explore interests and find productive avenues to relax. This time provides an opportunity to search for personal identity and purpose. It also establishes productive outlets to manage stress.

In order to implement Quiet Time, parents can set aside one hour for children to be in a *quiet,* non-stimulating environment. It is helpful to have Quiet Time at the same time each day. The key is to establish a period of time where a child's mind and body are exposed to low stimulus. This is a peaceful time to regroup, refresh, and recharge. Quiet Time encourages the use of imagination, productive behaviors, self-discipline, and self-entertainment. Quiet Time is not just for a child, parents can also use this time to explore interests, relax, and rejuvenate. It also provides down time to help buffer the physical demands of life.

 ## For Quiet Time

1. Determine a time of day your child can regularly enjoy Quiet Time.

2. Discuss the requirements of Quiet Time with your child. If you have more than one child, each one spends his Quiet Time *alone*.

   A. Quiet Time can be after lunch, after school, or in the evening.
   B. Use a Reminder Card to reinforce the importance of having Quiet Time.
   C. A timer can be used to indicate when Quiet Time ends. This helps eliminate constant questioning as to how much time remains. At first your child may resist Quiet Time, but once established, it will become a welcome time for both you and your child.

"My children are in school during the day so we have our Quiet Time in the evening from five to six. In the past this was a time when the house was chaotic and arguments often broke out. Now everyone has a chance to relax and focus on individual pursuits.

Quiet Time provides my children with an opportunity to step away from their hectic lives and refocus their energy on positive things. We have encouraged our children to use this opportunity to set goals, dream about the future, and seek out new interests.

I use this hour to pamper myself. Most of my day is spent caring for the others needs. Quiet Time is my time! I relax in a hot bath, read a good book, or  *just change into a fresh outfit. Now when my husband comes home I am refreshed and feel great!*

My husband typically arrives home before Quiet Time ends. This provides us with an opportunity to talk and enjoy each other's company in a relaxing setting. We both look forward to sharing our day and spending a few moments alone. My husband says that these moments help him shift gears and be ready to spend more focused time with the family." M.O.

HELPFUL HINT: Quiet Time is important at any age. If your child is young, Quiet Time will be his naptime. When your child no longer takes a nap, Quiet Time is an excellent transition that provides many of the same advantages.

"Our family has used Quiet Time for years. My younger children have learned that after lunch we all go to our rooms and spend one hour by ourselves. My children can read, listen to tapes, or play quietly. My children have all gone through periods where they do not nap, but they stay on their beds and play quietly during this time. It does take consistency and perseverance to establish this behavior, but the benefits are well worth it." R.Y.

Quiet Time Benefits

When children experience time alone and rely on simple, quiet activities for entertainment, they begin to use their imagination, develop self-discipline, and develop ways to manage stress in their lives.

It is necessary for your child to sit still and remain quiet at certain times. Quiet Time helps develop that ability. After your child has developed the habits associated with Quiet Time, you can use this principle outside your home. Your child can have Quiet Time at ceremonies, restaurants, or church services.

Quiet Time Ideas

> Books
> Quiet games
> Puzzles
> Drawing
> Homework
> Writing letters
> Coloring
> Music
> Books on tape
> Listening to stories

Mary has three children. The oldest boy is in school, and the two little ones are home with her. Mary has been observing Quiet Time in her home ever since the oldest informed her he did not need to take naps anymore. After lunch all the children were required to spend one hour in their rooms. Some napped, some didn't, but all of them received the rest and quiet they needed.

When the oldest boy started school, he began having Quiet Time after school or as dinner was prepared. Mary's son quickly learned to use Quiet Time to finish his homework so he had time to play with his friends.

Mary noticed that on the days her children missed Quiet Time, their home was not as peaceful, and the children argued and fought more. Quiet Time became Mary's favorite time of the day because she began using this hour to pamper herself by reading. Mary found she was more patient with her children and had more energy when she took Quiet Time for herself.

Quiet Time is For Everyone

How often do you take a full hour to indulge your interests, your needs, and your wants? Perhaps this is the time to start doing so. Turn off the phone, put aside the chores, and nourish yourself. The time you take will energize you for the busy evening to come.

You can spend your Quiet Time reading a book, taking a nap, arranging flowers, looking through a magazine, working on a scrapbook, taking pictures, writing letters, or sitting quietly in the swing. Ok . . . ok . . . some of you may be actually laughing, thinking this could never happen, but it can!

Claim your time today! Take time for yourself! If you are refreshed and do something you enjoy for one hour every day, you will have more patience, energy, and direction in your day.

One day Carol went to lunch with her friend Jane. They were talking about Jane's new pottery class. Jane had the new Community Catalog that listed different classes and invited Carol to look through the book to see if there was something she was interested in learning. Carol said she would love to take a class, but as she looked through the book, she started to cry. It had been so long since she had done something for herself, that she actually didn't know what she liked anymore.

Imagine that every day you carry a bucket of water with you. You can drink from the bucket and refill it at any time. Throughout the day you give everyone around you sips from your bucket, but you remain too busy to drink yourself. You give to others, while you collapse parched and weak from thirst. When this happens, you find yourself unable to give to anyone.

Quiet time is *your* time to fill your bucket with whatever you desire. Taking time for yourself is not being selfish. Your personal Quiet Time can help you be a better parent, spouse, and friend because now you will have something to give without feeling frustrated and empty. Let the washing, dishes, paper work, and phone calls wait for one hour. Give yourself the gift of Quiet Time and be renewed and refreshed. When you give to yourself, you will have more to give to those you love.

"Last week we attended a graduation ceremony for a good friend. Before we left, our children were told to take their Quiet Time bags. We discussed the specifics for receiving their Reminder Card.

During the ceremony, I noticed a mother in front of us was struggling to keep her children quiet and still. After the ceremony, a gentleman tapped me on the shoulder and asked how I was able to teach my children to be so well behaved. I just smiled and told him that it was a lot of love and consistency.

Quiet Time has been wonderful for our entire family. My children have developed the ability to quietly entertain themselves, and I have learned to take time for myself each day." M.N.

HELPFUL HINT: If you work outside your home, you may need to schedule your Quiet Time differently. You may decide to start waking up one hour early, plan time alone at lunchtime, or take one hour in the evening just for you. Let your family know your plans so they can support and encourage your time alone.

One day Elaine called her sister and said she had discovered the secret to life. Her sister was intrigued and wanted to know more. Elaine said that recently she had been struggling in her life. She felt she had been giving to everyone all day long and was worn out and depleted. In the past she used to do quite a bit for herself, but now that she had children, it was difficult to keep up with everything. Because of this, her needs came last.

Elaine said things changed about a month ago when she decided to wake up one hour before her children. She took this time to read the paper, wake up slowly, and enjoy quiet time by herself. Elaine said she couldn't believe the difference it was making in her life. When her kids woke up, she was glad to see them. She was ready for the day to begin and had more patience for her family.

Even though she was waking up earlier, Elaine felt more refreshed and less tired. She was finally taking time for herself and "filling her bucket" every day. She even discovered new interests. Her time alone allowed her to begin reading and enjoying books about photography. She is now planning on taking a class at the local college.

Tips for Quiet Time

> Make certain the room is child-proof.
> Check up on your child periodically to ensure compliance.
> Create a Quiet Time bag for you and your children with books, games, and quiet activities.
> Lead by setting a good example. Make your Quiet Time a priority.

Congratulations!! You have completed all four steps of the *Accountable Kids* program. You have learned the basic steps necessary to carry on the *AK* program in your home. Raising an Accountable kid is not easy. It takes work and consistency, but the rewards far outweigh the efforts. Although this seems like the ending, it is really just the beginning of an exciting journey.

Pay Now or Pay Later

There are various reasons to put off starting the *Accountable Kids* program, but many parents have learned the painful and expensive lesson that you can either "pay now or pay later". If parents don't take the time to teach, motivate, and encourage children today, they may be *forced* into this role later as their children struggle in school, work, and social settings.

Society pays the price as more youth are being placed in wilderness programs, residential treatment facilities, correctional institutions, tracking programs, and troubled youth homes. Life is complicated and busy, but the truth is we all have time for the things we consider priorities. *Accountable Kids* invites you to take the opportunity to make your child a *priority*. Give your child the gift of learning accountability and responsibility.

If childhood and adolescence is viewed as an apprenticeship to responsible adulthood, then what could be more powerful than teaching your child the benefits of hard work, accountability, self-worth, self-discipline, and family unity at a young age? Childhood and adolescence mark critical times to teach valuable principles and create a foundation from which your child can grow and develop. If your child develops a solid foundation based on love, respect, discipline, and consistency, she is more likely to manifest these traits later in life.

The *Accountable Kids* program does not shelter your child from all the pitfalls in life, but it teaches basic principles that, if learned and applied, will help your child develop important life skills that will continue into adulthood. These are the same basic skills by which successful, contributing adults live their lives.

Although most parents realize the benefits of implementing the *Accountable Kids* program in their home, some are hesitant to commit to the program because of time, money, effort, and lack of knowledge. Unfortunately, the consequence for not taking the time and effort to implement accountability may be insurmountable.

Society is experiencing an alarming increase in drug use, alcohol abuse, teen-age pregnancy, suicide, co-dependency, and gang affiliation. It is important for children to learn accountability when they are young. Parents who do not take the time to teach accountability to children at a young age, may pay a much higher price when their children mature.

Common Road Blocks

"I don't have the time!"

Parents that do not have the time to implement this program may want to reconsider how they spend their days. Adults spend an average of fifteen hours a week watching television (Robinson and Godbey, 1997). The average school age child spends twenty-one hours a week in front of the television. On the average, fathers spend only five focused minutes a day with their children, and mothers spend only twenty directed minutes (Covey, 1997).

Time is a limited resource for everyone. In the *AK* program children learn to contribute to the family and behave in positive ways, freeing up more time for positive interactions and activities with parents. Instead of spending time solving problems, parents and children can spend quality, fun time together. Children learn the direct correlation between limited resources and behaviors.

By providing children with time and attention, parents can change the way they develop and interact at home, school, and work. Initially the *AK* program will require planning, time, and dedication to implement, but very quickly children become responsible enough to manage the program on their own with only minimal guidance from parents. In the long run, the *AK* program will save parents time, because they are no longer directing every task children do.

Children will learn to accomplish chores without reminders or help from parents while using the *AK* program. Parents may actually see children looking for extra chores to do around the home to pay for more privileges. Children will learn not to argue with parents about purchasing items in stores because they are now responsible and empowered to purchase the items they desire. Children may also be more productive without *unlimited* television programs, video games, and talking on the phone. These activities are all *limited* within the program.

"The program seems complicated."

The *AK* program does have depth, but it is presented in four easy to follow steps. It begins with the basics and then incorporates additional components as children progress. Once parents understand the principles behind raising an *Accountable Kid*, the program will become second nature to them. Children will become responsible for completing chores, hanging Reminder Cards up, tallying earnings, and paying for privileges. Children will learn to perform and report; parents simply monitor progress.

"I don't want to reward my child for everything."

The *AK* program does not encourage a reward system that will teach children to grow up expecting something for every action. Positive behaviors are initially shaped and then sustained by altering the frequency of incentives.

The *Accountable Kids* program understands the principle that incentives are important for children to *begin* a new behavior, but continuous incentives are not required to *sustain* the behavior. Continuous incentives are only used until children learn to incorporate a new, positive behavior. At this point, the behavior will be strengthened using an intermittent reinforcement such as the Best Behavior Card. Finally, internal reinforcements will be stressed to develop a feeling of self-confidence and identity.

Children learn that their actions bring consequences, either positive or negative. Parents no longer determine what a child receives or is able to do. This results in a great feeling of empowerment. Parents are simply free to encourage and love. Children learn that actions determine consequences, and emotion is no longer a part of the process.

"My child is away from home all day."

Although many young children spend their days in day care or school, the *AK* program can still be very beneficial. Even if children are away from home most of the day, they still have responsibilities before and after school.

When children are away from home all day, it is even more important to provide structure and consistency in the home when they return. The *AK* program provides the tools for parents to establish an effective system where family members can maximize their time and efforts. Children learn exactly what is expected and understand the consequences of not fulfilling their obligations. The principles of the *AK* program provide structure and harmony to a hectic household.

"What is the harm in giving my child what I never had?"

Many parents want to give their children all the things they never had. But in doing this, parents often deprive children of the learning, development, struggle, and pain that helped them to become accountable adults. Children need to develop feelings of self-worth and self-empowerment and experience the accomplishment of struggling and working to complete goals. If children are given everything they need and want, they often grow up expecting the same gifts later in life.

The *AK* program teaches valuable lessons through work and play. Children learn that work can be fun, and chores are a necessary part of life. Many adolescents leave the home unprepared to take care of themselves and run a household. They were raised in a home that was cleaned by someone else, food magically appeared on the table, and there was always enough money for whatever they wanted.

Spoiled children are often raised with a sense of entitlement and are ill prepared to enter the workforce or maintain healthy relationships. Parents who always place the needs of their child above their own needs, create a child who believes his needs are the most important. This entitled child will continue to believe and expect that everyone else should make concessions or change rules to ensure his needs are met.

It is no wonder that so many young adults don't move out of the house . . . why would they? They are taken care of and do not have to provide for their needs. They have come to expect others to take care of them. It may feel wonderful to give your child all the things you did not have, but in doing so, do not exclude the necessary lessons, hard work, and struggle that will help your child develop into an accountable adult.

"There will be plenty of time for my child to work later."

We are who we are because of the learning and experiences we encounter. When a parent gives a child everything, the child is deprived of learning necessary life lessons. Children develop self-confidence, empowerment, and self-worth from accomplishing and achieving.

Childhood provides an opportunity to learn and develop. It provides a safety net for experiencing and failing. With proper support and encouragement, the failures of childhood can be directed toward learning and growth. Childhood is the time to learn the life lessons that will serve individuals throughout adulthood.

The *AK* program is structured to give children the basics of experiencing actions and consequences. The program is carried out in a safe environment where failure is monitored and children are able to learn from their mistakes and successes.

It is important for children to learn responsible independence. Parents who rescue their children and do not allow them to solve problems, enable them to avoid accountability at the expense of responsibility and independence.

The developmental stages of children focus on attributes such as initiative, industry, and identity that derive from learning new skills through work. Children who are not encouraged to help at a young age may not develop direction, competency, and purpose in life.

Questions & Answers

The following are some of the most frequently asked questions from parents using the *Accountable Kids* program. Hopefully, you can learn through these questions and take your journey to a higher level. If you have a question or story you would like to share with *Accountable Kids,* we would love to hear from you.

Q: We live in a busy household and our schedule changes from day to day. How can I use a structured program when it is necessary to continually direct my child during an unpredictable day?

A: The *AK* program provides a way for you to stop dictating every task your child performs. You learn to release control and teach your child to be responsible for his actions and consequences. The *AK* program does not give you more control over your child, but rather gives your child the ability to make appropriate decisions in order to better control himself. Your child learns to take control of his own life. This program will save you time as your child becomes more accountable and no longer requires your constant direction.

Q: My son currently receives an allowance. How do we make the transition into the *AK* program?

A: The *AK* program does not provide for an allowance. Children only receive what they earn. An allowance promises children a specific amount of money with the hope that they will perform certain chores. Parents are often placed in a difficult position of deciding how much allowance to take away for uncompleted jobs.

Since your child is already receiving an allowance, continue this arrangement during the first two steps of the program. When he is ready for the third step introducing Extra Chores and Savings, establish a new arrangement.

Explain to your son that he will no longer receive an allowance, but he will have the opportunity to make the same money, maybe even more. Let him know that he will now receive money in the form of Bonus Bucks each time an Extra Chore is completed. Once a week, his Bonus Bucks will be exchanged for real money. Discuss how Bonus Bucks are only earned if all his Core Chores are completed. Your son will earn money by completing Extra Chores and learn the importance of completing all his Core Chores.

Q: My oldest daughter often baby-sits for me. I don't currently pay her for this because I feel everyone in the family should work together to help one another. My daughter is starting to resent this job. Can the *AK* program help us?

A: Yes! You can pay your daughter for babysitting without it costing you additional money. Take a minute and consider all the things your daughter receives daily and weekly. Why not begin paying her for babysitting, but also allow her to begin paying for the items you are currently providing such as lessons, clothing, school activities, extra food, personal items, etc.

Present your daughter with a job proposal for babysitting. Establish a rate for her services, and explain that she will be responsible to record dates and hours worked. Take time to discuss your expectations for the job. Sign off on her records and disperse earnings weekly at the Family Forum. Allow your daughter to help purchase clothing, personal items, and individual activities with the money she earns.

This process allows for choice and consequence. Your daughter may decide that she doesn't want to take the job. In this case you may have to hire an outside person and deduct this money from the family budget. This will take resources away from your daughter. If your daughter experiences a deficit in her life, she will seek ways to fill it.

Q: My child has special needs, and I am not certain this program will work for her.

A: This program is easily tailored for a child with special needs. Use the program as outlined for the first four steps. Observe how your child adapts to the program, and then customize it to work with her individual needs.

Q: I am worried that my children are going to be competitive during this program and will not learn to cooperate.

A: If you have more than one child, avoid using challenges that have only one winner. The *AK* program stresses cooperation rather than competition. For example, if you would like your children to clean their rooms, have a contest where whoever has the room cleaned by a specific time earns an Extra Ticket, instead of awarding a Ticket to the first person that cleans his room. Teach children that family members work together, and the success of one member does not inhibit the success of another.

Discuss age appropriate tasks with your children. Each member of the family may be functioning in a different developmental stage. A four year old is not required to do the same job as a fourteen year old, but they are both required to put forth quality effort.

Q: We are a religious family, and Sunday is a day that we don't do chores. How do we use the *AK* program on the days that our children don't do chores?

A: Your children may not perform Extra Chores on Sunday, but they will still be responsible to accomplish basic Core Chores. If Sunday is a day of rest for your family, you may want to use this day to hold your Family Forum and prepare for the upcoming week.

Q: What do I do on the days that my child is sick?

A: Sick days are a time to rest and recuperate. Your child will not earn Tickets for chores or be able to use Tickets for fun activities (even if she has some saved from a previous day). This helps her understand that staying home from school is not a day of fun and playing. It is also helpful to remind your child that staying home from school  makes the entire day a sick day. Even if your daughter starts to feel better in the afternoon, she remains home and does not enjoy Ticketed Activities.

Q: One child is doing great with your system, but the other child is not motivated to do chores. What do we do?

A: Determine what your child is willing to work for by completing the Accountable Kids questions (Appendix D). Every child has wants and needs. It may be difficult to select the exact activities that motivate your child at a particular time because they may change. You may have to continually reassess Ticketed  Activities to keep your child motivated. This does not mean that you keep adding more and more to satisfy your child, it simply means you add, change, and offer variety.

Imagine going to the store every day and treating yourself to a chocolate ice cream cone. You may be willing to pay one dollar for the ice cream cone in the beginning, but after awhile you may not want to pay the same amount for another chocolate cone. (It may be hard to imagine having too much chocolate). You may want more ice cream, just another flavor.

Your child operates in the same manner. Pay attention to what motivates him. You can ask your child to suggest new incentives. Remember, if there is no deficit in your child's life, there will be little or no motivation driving him to reach goals and rewards. A child who has everything is seldom motivated to work.

Q: Today I discovered my son lied about completing a chore. What should I do?
A: Trust is an essential ingredient in the *AK* program. Your son becomes trustworthy by earning your trust. This occurs at different levels depending on the cognitive development of your child. If your child is preoperational, he is still learning about good and bad, true and false, and right and wrong. The focus should be on teaching your child the difference between these concepts. An operational child should know the difference between right and wrong. Consider your child's developmental stage, and then assign an age appropriate consequence.

Q: We use timeouts as a discipline measure, and generally I only have to count to three and my son responds. Can I keep doing this in the *AK* program?
A: Many parents use forms of discipline that do not work as the child develops physically and mentally. Taking Tickets is a form of discipline that will grow with

your child and closely resembles real world consequences.

Productive adults have learned that fun activities come after responsibilities are met and they pay the price for privileges and activities. Children using the *AK* program also learn that privileges and activities are earned with positive behavior and can be taken away for negative behavior. Accountable children learn that positive behaviors provide more benefits than negative behaviors.

Discipline should be immediate and impact your child. Warn your child once, and if the behavior is repeated, take a Ticket. Counting to three simply teaches your son that he doesn't need to respond the first time you ask. To eliminate a negative behavior, stop giving multiple warnings. You are *encouraging* your child to perform the negative behavior if you find yourself saying the following statements:

If you say
If I tell you one more time. . .
What part of "No" do you not
    understand?
I am not going to tell you again!
How many times do I have to tell you?
I mean it this time!
One more time, and I'll . . .

Replace it with
Please give me a Ticket.

Q: My child is always arguing with me. How do I change her behavior?
A: This is a common problem for parents. The purpose of the *AK* program is to create an environment where a

child learns to make choices and become accountable for those choices. After the program has been established in your home, your child should know exactly what is expected and appropriate on a daily basis. Arguing at this point becomes manipulation. Each time you allow your child to argue, you are encouraging this behavior in the future. Establish firm consequences for such actions, and then be consistent and unwavering.

If rules need to be changed, the Family Forum is a good place to talk about it. This way, you are discussing ideas rather than specific problems.

Q: Can I just use part of the program?
A: Before you decide that certain components of the *AK* program won't work, it is helpful to follow the established Four Step program to test all the components. Too often parents have preconceptions of what won't work and miss out on wonderful learning opportunities. You may even learn new ways to motivate and teach your child accountability if you implement the entire program.

Q: Can one child share Tickets with another? My young daughter uses all her Tickets before her brothers come home from school. She then feels sad when she can't watch a movie or play a game with them. My oldest son wants to give his sister a Ticket so she can play with them. Should I let him do this?
A: Although this would be a great gesture from your son, it may actually encourage irresponsible behavior in your daughter in the long run. If your daughter is in the operational stage of development, she is capable of planning ahead and should be allowed to make choices and experience consequences.

Preoperational children have difficulty understanding the passage of time and may not budget time and resources. Try structuring your day so that your daughter earns a Ticket around the time her brother comes home from school. This way she gets to experience an activity with her brother and learns the value of earning a Ticket at this time of the day.

Q: I have several children, but only one child is giving me problems. Can I use the *AK* program for just one child?

A: Unless your child is too young to use the *AK* program, include all children. This program is not just for children with problems. It can be beneficial and enjoyable for all children, regardless of their specific needs.

Q: I have been using the *AK* program for a few months with tremendous success. My children are now doing their Core Chores without reminders and completing Extra Chores to earn spending money. I would like know if the *AK* program also provides opportunities to teach the benefits of helping others through service.

A: Yes, the Helping Hands Card, which is discussed in Chapter Seven, can help your children experience the rewards of service. This Reminder Card encourages your children to seek out ways to help others each day and provides an avenue for parents to ask their children for help without being questioned for monetary rewards. The Helping Hands Card provides a unique reminder for your children to focus on other people and look for ways to better not only the family, but also neighbors and the community.

Q: My child is only two years old. How do I know when to start using this program?

A: Learning the different stages of development can be beneficial for all parents (Refer to Chapter Three). The entire *AK* program can be started when a child begins to associate actions with consequences. This usually occurs somewhere between two and three years of age. Parents can utilize parts of the program at a younger age if they want to focus on specific age related attributes or learn more about the development of their child.

The *AK* program is presented in four steps. Each step introduces a new phase until the entire program is incorporated. Young children may stay on the first step for several months. The next step is introduced once a child understands and demonstrates the concepts of the current step.

Q: My children fight all the time. How can I get them to get along?

A: Start by taking Tickets every time your children fight. It is possible to change behavior, but it is not easy nor immediate. The authors of *The Discipline Book* state, "As you weed out the undesirable behaviors one by one, your child gradually gets used to the feelings that come with good behavior, and these feelings become self-motivating" (Sears and Sears, 1995).

Effective discipline teaches your child that negative behaviors have negative consequences for them. It is therefore important to teach character traits that develop internal values and integrity.

Q: Our family travels frequently. How do we use this program while away from home?

A: The *AK* program can travel easily with your family if you establish rules, responsibilities, and consequences while away from home. Optional travel accessories are available to help you continue the program as you travel.

Q: We are finding it difficult to use the program on a consistent basis. It just seems too much for us to fit this program into our busy life.

A: Consistency is important to the success of the *AK* program. One way to remain committed to the program is by regularly holding your Family Forum. Each week presents an opportunity for you and your children to work together to maximize and strengthen the program.

It takes time and effort to get the *AK* program running consistently, but once your child develops accountability for behaviors and chores, this program will save you time. However, in the beginning, you will have to put forth time and effort and be willing to allow your child to experience choices and consequences.

Q: My son always has plenty of Tickets. I forget to charge Tickets throughout the day, so taking Tickets as a form of discipline doesn't work.

A: Tickets are secondary reinforcements. They do not possess a value unless attached to something. If you don't charge Tickets for Ticketed Activities, your child will not value this incentive. Encourage your child to use Tickets and pay for activities to establish value.

The *AK* program reinforces the relationship between actions and consequences. It is up to you to teach this life lesson. Teach your child to pay for privileges before they can be enjoyed. You can establish a rule that an extra Ticket will be charged if your child enjoys a privilege without paying for it. This shifts the responsibility from you to your child.

Q: Can I use this program for my teenager?
A: Yes, the *AK* program begins teaching children in a basic and simple format, but the components are designed to grow with your child. If your child is starting this program as a teenager, you will still begin with the basic program until positive patterns of accountability are established.

An older child will learn the principles more quickly than a younger child, but he may express more resistance to the program. You can expand and incorporate the components of the program to match the progress of your child. The principles introduced in the basic program provide the foundation for your child to progress to the next level of accountability where contracts and verbal agreements are implemented.

Q: Isn't this just another chore chart program? Our family has done a chore chart program in the past. The program worked for a few months, but then my children got tired of it.

A: Many parents have been unsuccessful using chore charts, however the *AK* program is much more than a basic charting system. The *AK* program presents a program with depth, growth potential, and flexibility that will work with you today and in the future.

Most chore charts focus entirely on getting a child to complete chores. The *Accountable Kids* program implements components in a specific manner that encourages children to display desirable behaviors and eliminate negative behaviors. A specific reinforcement process is used to produce long-term benefits.

This program develops work ethics as well as character. It is unique in that it teaches parents and children to become accountable for their actions today and in the future.

Q: My children earn their bath Reminder Card after bathing, putting their clothes in the hamper, and wiping water off the floor. Generally, they only take a bath every other day, so I take down the bath Reminder Card on no bathing days.

On a no bathing day my son was particularly dirty and required a bath. After his bath he did not put his clothes in the hamper. I told him he would not earn a Ticket for taking a bath, and thus his Evening Chores were not complete. This meant he would not receive a sticker for the Special Date Card. He objected because the bathing card was not on the Progress Board that day. He believed he should still receive a Ticket and sticker for completing all of his Core Chores. What would be a good solution to our problem?

A: First, stop taking Reminder Cards on and off the Progress Board every day. This program is supposed to simplify your life, not add more work. Leave the Core Chores on the board and excuse any chores that do not have to be completed.

Your child was taught he would receive a Ticket if all the evening chores were completed. Taking a bath was not a Core Chore for this day because you removed it from the Progress Board. He successfully completed all of his Core Chores and should receive a Ticket and sticker, however you can charge your son a Ticket for having to pick up his clothes.

Q: We have been using the *Accountable Kids* program in our home for several months. It works well when I am home, but my husband struggles to charge Tickets for activities. He is not consistent with the program because he does not remember what activities require a Ticket and what behaviors cause a Ticket to be taken.

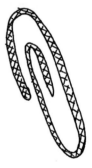

A: It is important for all adults and children in the home to understand and consistently use the *Accountable Kids* program. Your husband can refer to the *Fast Track to Accountable Kids* located in Appendix F to learn the basics of the program. It may help if you post reference sheets to remind everyone what activities require a Ticket. Appendix E contains forms that will help you specify Ticketed Activities, indicate time limits, and describe behaviors that will cost your child a Ticket.

If you take the time to complete these forms, the program runs smoother.

This program is designed to teach your child to be accountable for choices and consequences. Your child is responsible to move Reminder Cards, ask for earned Tickets, and give you a Ticket for Ticketed Activities. You have a responsibility to teach your child the *AK* program, but then you should only be monitoring your child's progress.

Q: Sometimes I want to give my child a gift. Does the AK program provide for gift giving?
A: The *AK* program focuses on teaching children to earn what they receive, but giving and receiving gifts can be a great experience and a wonderful part of life. Even adults appreciate gifts when they are given unexpectedly and occasionally. It is not necessary for a child to earn everything in life. Giving gifts to a child can be fun and rewarding, but a gift is not a gift when it is expected. If a child begins to expect items, eliminate gift giving until the expectations change. If gifts are received with appreciation, then gift giving can be a good experience for everyone.

Appendix

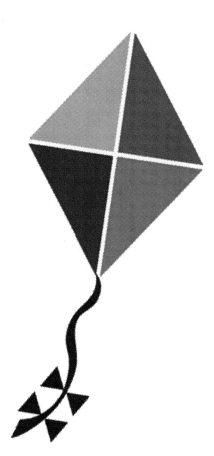

References and Suggested Reading

Ammerman, T. T., & Hersen, M. (1995). Handbook of child behavior therapy in the psychiatric setting. New York: Wiley.

Bennett, W. J. (1998). Our country's founders. New York: Simon & Schuster Books for Young Readers.

Bijour, S. W. (1976). Child development: The basic stage of early childhood. Englewood Cliffs, NJ: Prentice Hall.

Cline, F., & Fay, J. (1990). Parenting with love and logic. Colorado Springs, Colorado: Pinion Press.

Covey S. R. (1997). The 7 habits of highly effective families. New York: Golden Books Publishing.

Crain, W. C. (1980). Theories of development: concepts and applications. Englewood Cliffs, New Jersey: Prentice-Hall, Inc.

Eyre, L., & Eyre, R. (1994). Three steps to a strong family. New York: Simon and Schuster.

Gray, J. (2001). Children are from heaven. New York: HarperCollins Publishers Inc.

Jones, J. J. (1997). Let's fix the kids. Self Publish.

Kohlberg, L. (1963). The development of children's orientations toward a moral order: I. Sequence in the development of moral thought. Vata Humana, 6, 11-33

Kohn, A. (1993). Punished by rewards. New York: Houghton Mifflin Company

Locke, J. (1963). Some thoughts concerning education. P. Gay (Ed.), John Locke on Education. New York: Bureau of Publications, Teacher's College, Columbia University, 1964

Neufeldt, V., & Guralnik, D. B. (ed.). (1996). Websters new world college dictionary. (3rd ed.). New York: Macmillan.

MacGregor, C. (2000). Fun family traditions. Minnetonka, Minnesota: Meadowbrook Press.

McGraw J. (2002). Life Strategies for teens. New York: Fireside.

Phillips, J. L. (1981). Piaget's Theory: A Primer. San Francisco: W.H. Freeman and Company

Robinson J. P., & Godbey G. (1997). Time for life. University Park, Pennsylvania: The Pennsylvania State University Press.

Schlessinger, L. (2000). Stupid things parents do to mess up their kids. New York: HarperCollins.

Sears, W., & Sears, M. (1995). The discipline book: everything you need to know to have a better-behaved child-from birth to age ten. Canada: Little, Brown & Company.

Reminder Cards

Reminder Cards	Graphic	Suggested Uses
Clean room	Bedroom	Picking up room
Make Bed	Bed made up	Making bed
Brush teeth	Tooth brush, tooth paste, cup	Brushing teeth in the morning, flossing teeth
Brush teeth	Tooth brush, tooth paste, cup	Brushing teeth in the evening, flossing teeth
Bath	Old fashioned tub with shower head	Bathing, showering, washing up
Pick up toys	Assortment of toys	Clean room, clean playroom, pick up toys
Vitamins	Two bottles and pills	Taking vitamins or medication
Get dressed	Shirt, pants, sock, shoes	Putting clothes on, laying clothes out
Hair Care	Hair dryer, brush, and comb	Doing hair
Pajamas	Pajamas	Putting on pjs, getting ready for bed
Dirty Clothes	Dirty clothes in basket	Putting dirty clothes in hamper, washing clothes
Breakfast	Plate with eggs, bacon & toast	Eating breakfast, helping with breakfast, morning activity
Lunch	Sandwich, milk, snack	Eating lunch, helping with lunch, packing lunch for school, afternoon activity
Dinner	Plate of spaghetti	Eating dinner, helping with dinner, evening activity
Car Ride	Picture of car	Putting seatbelt on, good behavior in the car, getting ready to go in the car

Pet Care	Assortment of animals	Feeding, bathing, walking, maintenance
Mail	Mail box	Bringing in mail or paper
Quiet Time	Moon with night cap	Spending time in a non-stimulating manner
Prayers	Child kneeling down to pray	Saying prayers
Church	Church building	Attending church, going to a spiritual activity
Scriptures	Bible with oil lamp	Reading religious material
Laundry	Washer and dryer	Washing clothes, folding clothes
Vacuum	Picture of vacuum	Vacuuming
Prepare Meals	Food, pots, pans, utensils	Preparing a meal, helping clean up
Trash	Inside garbage can	Emptying the inside garbage cans
Flag	American flag	Putting flag up, taking flag down, saying the pledge of allegiance
Plant Care	Potted plants	Watering or care of inside plants
Dust	Duster	Dusting the home
Mop	Mop and water bucket	Cleaning the floors
Sweep	Broom, dust pan	Cleaning the floors
Yard work	Rake, shovel, hose	Weeding, mowing lawn, watering, care of garden, outside help
Clear Table	Plate with food, pots, food plates	Clearing table, washing dishes
Set Table	Place setting	Setting the table for a meal
Dishes	Sink with bubbles, dishes	Washing dishes or putting dishes in the dishwasher
Cleaning	Spray bottle, rag, soap, cleaner	Any type of cleaning
Clean Bathroom	Bathroom with cleaning supplies	Cleaning bathroom, tidying bathroom
Music	Sheet of music with bluebird	Practicing any type of music
Recycle	Red arrows with recycled material in middle	Putting recycled material in appropriate place, emptying recycle bins
Sun Protection	Sun with glasses	Putting sunscreen on, wearing hat or glasses

166

Personal Items	Coat rack with hat, shoes	Putting away personal items, getting personal items ready for school
School	Backpack with apple and book	Setting out items for school, good report from school, putting school items away, bringing home school items
On Time	Clock with numbers	Getting up on time, going to bed on time, coming home on time, leaving the home on time
Reading	Books	Personal reading, homework
Homework	Desk, computer, & books	Completing homework
Lawn Care	Lawn mower	Mow lawn, edging, watering lawn
Shovel Snow	Snowman and snow shovel	Snow removal, wearing coat, bringing coat home from school
Helping Hands	Heart with hands	Helping others, community service, Extra Chores that do not receive pay
Morning	Sunrise	Multiple morning chores, good behavior for the morning, getting up without problems
Day	Sun	Multiple day chores or good behavior for the day
Evening	Moon with stars	Multiple evening chores, good behavior for the night, going to bed without problems

Sample Kids Program

Aly-5 years old
First Stage

Morning (Yellow)	Day (Red)	Evening (Blue)	Extra Jobs (Green & Purple)
Brush teeth Get dressed Make Bed Clean Room Take Vitamins	Quiet Time Pick up toys	Take Bath Pajamas Clean Room Brush Teeth Read Books Say Prayers	Optional
Constant	Constant	Constant	Optional
1 Ticket	1 Ticket	1 Ticket	Bonus Buck

Second Stage

Aly is assigned daily and weekly Extra Chores that can rotate periodically. Basic Reminder Cards are removed and existing cards redefined to include the removed chore. This combines two or more tasks into one Reminder Card. Helping Hands becomes a Core Chore.

Morning (Yellow) Daily	Day (Red) Daily	Evening (Blue) Daily	Extra Chore (Purple) Daily	Extra Chore (Green) Weekly
Brush teeth Get dressed Clean Room Take Vitamins	Helping Hands Quiet Time Pick up toys Feed Dog Get mail	Pajamas Clean Room Brush Teeth Read Books Say Prayers	Set Table	Garbage Yard work
Constant	Constant	Constant	Rotates	Rotates
1 Ticket	1 Ticket	1 Ticket	1 Bonus Buck	1 Bonus Buck

Blake-10 years old
First Stage

Morning (Yellow)	Day (Red)	Evening (Blue)	Extra Chores Daily (Purple)	Extra Chores Weekly (Green)
Brush teeth Get dressed Make Bed Take Vitamins	Personal items School Homework Piano	Pajamas Clean Room Brush Teeth Make Lunch Reading Say Prayers	Optional	Optional
Constant	Constant	Constant	Rotates	Rotates
1 Ticket	1 Ticket	1 Ticket	1 Bonus Buck	1 Bonus Buck

Second Stage

Blake is assigned daily and weekly Extra Chores that can rotate periodically. Basic Reminder Cards are replaced by Morning, Day, and Evening Cards. One Chore Card now represents several chores. Helping Hands is added as a Core Chore. A Separate list of specific Extra Chores is posted for additional opportunities.

Morning (Yellow)	Day (Red)	Evening (Blue)	Extra Jobs Daily (Purple)	Extra Jobs Weekly (Green)
Morning Card	Personal items School Report Homework Piano	Evening Card Helping Hands Make Lunch Reading	Dishes Sweep floor	Clean Bathroom Dust Vacuum
Constant	Constant	Constant	Rotates	Rotates
1 Ticket	1 Ticket	1 Ticket	1 Bonus Buck	1 Bonus Buck

Accountable Kids
Questions for Parents

Responsibilities
1. List the tasks your child completes every morning, afternoon, and evening.
2. List the chores your child is **not** currently doing, but you would like to see completed daily.
3. How many times a day do you remind your child to complete basic chores?

Tickets
1. List all the activities and privileges your child enjoys.
2. List any activities you would like to limit in your child's day.

Best Behavior Card
1. What values or virtues would you like your child to develop?
2. List the positive behaviors your child exhibits.
3. What is your current way of acknowledging positive behaviors?

Discipline
1. What is your current form of discipline?
2. Will your current discipline program be effective in five years?

Special Date
1. List special activities you believe your child would enjoy doing with you.

Privilege Pass
1. List activities your child would consider extra special.
2. List specific negative behaviors your child is exhibiting that are disrupting the family.
3. Select one negative behavior you would like to eliminate.

Extra Jobs
1. List all the things your child is currently receiving without paying for them.
2. List the items for which your child currently pays.
3. List the daily extra chores your child could do to earn money.
4. List the weekly extra chores your child could do to earn money.
5. List the large expenses your child will have in the future.

Accountable Kids
Questions for Children

1. What are your favorite things to do during the day?
2. What activities would you consider extra special?
3. When you get in trouble what happens?
4. If you could go on a special date with a parent, what would you plan?
5. What things would you like to buy (large or small)?

Accountable Kids Forms

Good Job

Chore:_____

Completed when:

_____

_____

_____

_____

Accountable Kids

Reminder Card

Accountable Kids

Reminder Card:

_____

I have earned my Reminder Card when:

_____

_____

_____

_____

Ticketed Activities

Activity _____ # of

♥

♥

♥

♥

♥

♥

♥

♥

♥

Best Behavior

Best Behavior Cards are earned for:

♥

♥

♥

♥

♥

♥

♥

♥

♥

Tickets Lost

Negative Behavior   **# of Tickets**

♥

♥

♥

♥

♥

♥

♥

♥

Special Date Log

Participants	Activity	Date

♥

♥

♥

♥

♥

♥

♥

♥

♥

Privilege Pass

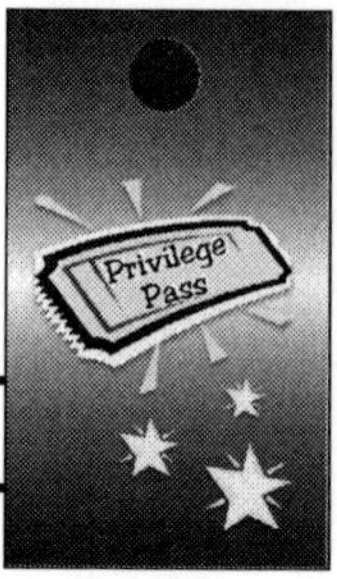

♥ **Target Positive Behavior**

_____

_____

_____

_____

Privilege Pass can be used for:

♥

♥

♥

♥

♥

♥

♥

♥

♥

♥

My Extra Chores

Name:

Date:

Daily Extra Chores:

♥

♥

♥

♥

♥

Weekly Extra Chores:

♥

♥

♥

♥

Hired Help

Job Completed By	Job Completed For	Price
♥		
♥		
♥		
♥		
♥		
♥		
♥		
♥		
♥		
♥		

Opportunity List

Job and Requirements	$$	Completed By

Passport
Savings Book

Date	Description	Amount	Balance

Things to Talk About in Family Forum

Topic _____ Presented by _____

♥

♥

♥

♥

♥

♥

♥

♥

Personal Progress

Name: _____

Date: _____

♥ Current Responsibilities

_____
_____
_____
_____
_____

♥ Achievements

_____
_____
_____
_____

♥ Goals

_____
_____
_____
_____

Accountable Kids

Family Forum Agenda

Date: _____

Parent in charge of meeting: _____

Activity Director: _____

Value of the Week: _____

New Rules:

_____

_____

Chore Assignments:

_____

_____

_____

_____

Wish List:

_____

_____

Misc:

_____

_____

_____

_____

_____

Page 1

Family Forum Agenda

1. Accountable Kids

2. Schedules

3. Problems & Solutions

4. Family Rules

5. Finances

6. Values and Virtues

Family Rules

♥ _____

_____

_____

_____

_____

_____

_____

_____

_____

_____

_____

_____

_____

_____

_____

_____

_____

_____

_____

_____

_____

_____

_____

_____

Accountable-Kids

To Accountable Kids

The *Fast Track to Accountable Kids* is provided for parents, grandparents, and care-givers as a quick reference. It contains the basic guidelines for implementing the *AK* program. It includes a Special Care Instructions form to provide specific information about your child. The *Fast Track* does not go into detail about how and why to implement the various components of the *AK* program, it is simply presented as a guide.

Step 1

Reminder Cards

➢ Reminder Cards represent Core Chores and Extra Chores.

➢ Reminder Cards with yellow, red, and blue bars on bottom are Core Chores. Core Chores are the child's responsibility every day.

➢ Morning Chores will have a yellow bar on the bottom, Day Chores will have a red bar on the bottom, and Evening Chores will have a blue bar on the bottom.

➢ The starting order for each day is: Evening Chores (blue) on bottom, the Day Chores (red) next, and the Morning Chores (yellow) on the top.

➢ Chores can be completed in any order within a color grouping.

➢ Each morning the *AK* Board is reset, and the Reminder Cards are moved to the Start Peg.

Tickets

Earning Tickets

➢ Children earn Tickets for completing Core Chores.

➢ The Reminder Card is moved to the Finish Peg as soon as the job is completed.

➢ One Ticket is earned if all the Morning Chores are completed, one Ticket is earned if all the Day Chores are completed, and one Ticket is earned if all the Evening Chores are completed (three possible Tickets).

- All of the chores in one color grouping must be completed to receive a Ticket for that color grouping.
- The card is rotated to the back of the pile and turned around if a chore is not completed.
- The child earns a Ticket immediately after completing one color grouping of chores.

Using Tickets
- Tickets are used to buy activities and privileges.
- A Ticket is charged for all Ticketed Activities.

Losing Tickets
- Tickets are taken for negative behaviors.
- When a Ticket is lost, ask for the explanation of why.
- Second chances are not given.

Best Behavior Cards
- The Best Behavior Card is given periodically to encourage positive behaviors and values.
- The Best Behavior Card is not given if it is requested.
- Best Behavior Cards are used as Tickets or placed in a special bag for a drawing.

Step 2

The Special Date Card
- A sticker is earned for the Special Date Card each day all of the basic Core Chores (Morning, Day, and Evening Chores) are completed.

➤ A Special Date is earned when all ten boxes are filled with stickers.

Privilege Pass

➤ The Privilege Pass is earned for displaying a specific positive behavior.
➤ The Privilege Pass can be used to buy an extra special privilege.

Extra Chores

➤ Extra Chore Reminder Cards have a purple or green bar on the bottom.
➤ Extra Chores are hung on the Extra Chore peg of the *AK* Board.
➤ The Extra Chore Card is moved to the Finish Peg when the job is completed.
➤ Extra Chores are encouraged any time of the day.

Bonus Bucks

➤ <u>Tickets</u> are earned for <u>Core Chores</u>, and <u>Bonus Bucks</u> are earned for <u>Extra Chores</u>.
➤ Bonus Bucks are dispersed at the end of the day.
➤ Bonus Bucks are only given if all of the Core Chores are completed.
➤ Bonus Bucks are exchanged for real money once a week.
➤ Earned money is divided into savings and personal spending.

Step 4

Family Forum

- ➢ A weekly meeting is held to discuss schedules, finances, problems and solutions, and individual progress.
- ➢ Each person is involved during the meeting.
- ➢ Keep meetings short, focused, and fun!
- ➢ Exchange Bonus Bucks for money, discuss upcoming special dates, and celebrate achievements.

Quiet Time

- ➢ Quiet Time is one hour of low stimulus.
- ➢ Have Quiet Time every day.
- ➢ A timer can be set to indicate when Quiet Time is over.

Handle with Care

LOVE

Instructions for the Accountable Kids Program

My Core Chores

Morning (Yellow) _____

Day (Red) _____

Evening (Blue) _____

My Extra Chores

Daily (Purple)

_____

_____

Weekly (Green)

_____

_____

Tickets can be used for

_____

_____

_____

Tickets are taken for

_____

_____

_____

Our Free Day is _____
I earn the Privilege Pass for

_____

_____

Our value of the week is _____
Our family meets on _____ for Family Forum.

Accountable Kids

Page 1

Handle with Care

Important Information

Where I can be reached

_____

_____

In case of emergency contact

_____

Our trusted neighbor

_____

Our Doctor

_____

Allergies or medications

_____

_____

Special Instructions

_____

_____

_____

_____

_____

_____

_____

_____

_____

Page 2

Accountable Kids
Reminders

1. Positive behaviors are started with continuous reinforcements and sustained using intermittent reinforcement.
2. Consistency develops habits.
3. Unconditional love is essential.
4. Positive behaviors can be shaped.
5. Negative behaviors are eliminated with negative consequences.
6. Inspire not require.
7. If you say it, do it.
8. Encourage instead of praise.
9. Continually reassess child's motivation.
10. Privileges are earned not given.
11. Children learn responsibilities by experiencing responsible behaviors.
12. Children choose actions, not consequences.

Authors' Note

Accountable Kids was created, not because we had all the answers, but because we had many of the same questions as other parents. We began searching for a program to teach our children accountability, responsibility, and integrity by sifting through the volumes of parenting books and manuals, and reading information with quick fixes and modern psychobabble. Many books offered opinions on how to parent effectively, but few offered the "nuts and bolts" or the step by step instructions with their theories. We also found that most books did not address the values and morals we believed needed to be at the core of our child rearing. We decided to unite our efforts and design a unique program for our children.

Accountable Kids represents the combined knowledge of Scott's fifteen years working with adolescents and a master's degree in marriage and family therapy, along with Traci's practicality and insight as a mother of three children. We have incorporated valuable lessons taught to us by our parents, as well as information gleaned from countless other parents and professionals who work with children on a daily basis.

As we developed the *Accountable Kids* program and observed the positive effect it had in our home, we decided to share this unique system with family and friends. In so doing, we discovered that *Accountable Kids* was the solution that other families were seeking. We also noticed that the program was not only beneficial to families with young children like ours, but it proved effective with children reaching into their teenage years.

What started out as a way to create a more harmonious family life in our home, grew into a complete parenting program suitable for other parents and children. It has been fun to see how this program has simplified our lives, helping our entire family be more productive.

We have both learned more than we could ever imagine over the past few years. Our program is finally finished . . . but we both know it is only the beginning. As our children grow, so will we. Several other books are in the creative process at the present time, and who knows where this journey of discovery and learning will take us. One thing we do know for certain: family, children, and love are our life priorities. All the decisions we make, all the things we do, and all the actions we take will center around teaching and raising Accountable Kids.

Scott and Traci Heaton

THE BEGINNING...

This program is not for every child. If you find your child has no desire to participate in the program, there may be underlying problems associated with his behaviors. Some behavior problems are complex enough that they require the assistance of a trained, behaviorally oriented clinical psychologist. If this is the case, it is recommended you seek professional help before using the *AK* program.